Homer: A Very Short Introduction

Praise for the hardback, *Homer*

'The perfect introduction to Homer.'

Times Literary Supplement

'Homer has flourished through millennia of cultural receptions, ending up (as Nietzsche noted) more like an "aesthetic judgment" than an historical fact. Barbara Graziosi in this highly readable, svelte volume offers a lucid and learned introduction that is characteristically attuned to key moments in the afterlife of the *Iliad* and *Odyssey*. Not only do we get a sensitive and fresh survey of the poems themselves and their ancient contexts (including roots in oral tradition, relationships with Near Eastern literature, and the evidence for a Trojan War). She also renews our awareness of the later impact of this earliest Greek literature, from Vergil to Primo Levi. Rich in detailed readings and packed with hints for further exploration, Graziosi's book provides the most up-to-date and reliable guide to the appreciation of two eternally relevant epics.'

Richard P. Martin, Antony and Isabelle Raubitschek Professor in Classics, Stanford University

'Authoritative, lucid, contemporary and exciting. Nobody writes for the public about Homer better than Barbara Graziosi.'

Edith Hall, Professor of Classics, King's College London

'This book rewards the general reader with a lively introduction to Homeric poetry—and to the artistic world in which this poetry originally came to life. Throughout her forceful exposition, the author does not hesitate to track her own critical views on the lasting value of reading Homer in our own time.'

Gregory Nagy, Francis Jones Professor of Classical Greek Literature, Harvard University, and Director of the Harvard Center for Hellenic Studies

VERY SHORT INTRODUCTIONS are for anyone wanting a stimulating and accessible way into a new subject. They are written by experts, and have been translated into more than 45 different languages.

The series began in 1995, and now covers a wide variety of topics in every discipline. The VSI library currently contains over 550 volumes—a Very Short Introduction to everything from Psychology and Philosophy of Science to American History and Relativity—and continues to grow in every subject area.

Very Short Introductions available now:

Available soon:

For more information visit our website

www.oup.com/vsi/

Barbara Graziosi

HOMER

A Very Short Introduction

Great Clarendon Street, Oxford, OX2 6DP,
United Kingdom

Oxford University Press is a department of the University of Oxford.
It furthers the University's objective of excellence in research, scholarship,
and education by publishing worldwide. Oxford is a registered trade mark of
Oxford University Press in the UK and in certain other countries

Published in the United States of America by Oxford University Press
198 Madison Avenue, New York, NY 10016, United States of America

British Library Cataloguing in Publication Data
Data available

Library of Congress Control Number: 2018962712

ISBN 978-0-19-958994-4

Printed in Great Britain by
Ashford Colour Press Ltd, Gosport, Hampshire

Contents

Acknowledgements

This book was written while directing a research project entitled *Living Poets: A New Approach to Ancient Poetry* <https://livingpoets.dur.ac.uk/>. I am grateful to the European Research Council for funding that project, and thus giving me and others the opportunity to investigate how, through the centuries, readers imagined the poets of Greece and Rome, and how in turn the biographies and portraits they produced served as introductions to the poets' works. I am grateful to Oxford University Press, and specifically commissioning editor Andrea Keegan, for giving me the opportunity to introduce Homer to readers today, starting with how he was imagined.

I would like to thank the anonymous peer reviewers for their expertise and encouragement: their comments improved the book in many ways. I have also benefitted from discussing Homer with Johannes Haubold over the years: many of the views presented here are the result of those conversations. Reading the *Iliad* and the *Odyssey* with students has been an important source of pleasure and insight, and proved especially useful when planning this book. David Elmer helped me track down the photograph on p. 16. Massimo Brizzi drew the maps on pp. 35 and 48. Kim Birchall prepared the Index and Mohana Annamalai oversaw production. I am very grateful for their expertise and patience. Emma Ma and Jenny Nugee at Oxford University Press offered unfailing support during the exceedingly long gestation of this very short book.

List of illustrations

Introduction

In 1354, Petrarch received a manuscript of the *Iliad* from a
Byzantine correspondent, and wrote to him in acknowledgement:

> Your Homer is mute to me. Or rather, I am deaf to him. Still,
> I rejoice even to look at him and often, as I embrace him,
> I say, sighing, 'O Great Man, how ardently would I listen to you!'

With this paradoxical love for an author he could not read,
Petrarch set in motion an intellectual movement of vast
proportions: the recovery of ancient Greek literature shaped
the Renaissance, or 'rebirth' of antiquity, and this early declaration
of love for Homer was one of its symbolic beginnings.

Petrarch did not content himself with hugging his incomprehensible
Homeric manuscript, but looked for a scholar who could translate
it, and teach him Greek along the way. He also helped to persuade
the City Fathers of Florence to establish the first chair of Greek in
Western Europe. Unfortunately, the man chosen for the position,
Leontius Pilate, proved to be unsuitable. Petrarch's letters reveal
something of the impression he made: 'stubborn', 'vain', 'volatile',
'badly dressed'. As disastrous academic appointments go, that of
Leontius Pilate must rank among the worst in history—and yet
the slow uptake of Greek in Western Europe was not just a result
of his poor manners or dress sense. Petrarch shared with his

Italian contemporaries an attitude of suspicion and superiority towards Byzantine culture, which was not conducive to language acquisition. He was more interested in making contact, directly, with Homer, than in learning the intricacies of Greek grammar.

Today, Homer's poems are easily accessible. A list of translations, published in 2003, runs to hundreds of pages, and includes all major modern languages, as well as Esperanto and several dialects and forms of *patois*. There are also countless grammars, commentaries, dictionaries, encyclopaedias, monographs, articles, and digital resources which greatly facilitate access to the *Iliad* and the *Odyssey* in the original Greek. Last but not least, there are many excellent teachers. And yet people today often find themselves in a position which resembles that of Petrarch: they assume that Homer is a great poet, but have not read any of the poetry attributed to him. Homeric epic still reaches us primarily through echoes and refractions in other poems, novels, plays, and works of art—as well as through the ubiquitous myth of the author, since everybody knows that there is a question about the identity, and even existence, of Homer himself.

Given the situation, this book has two main aims. The first is to facilitate an understanding of the *Iliad* and the *Odyssey*, by providing a succinct and up-to-date guide to the main literary, historical, cultural, and archaeological issues at the heart of Homeric studies. The second is to show, by way of concrete example, how readers of Homer join a vast and diverse community of other readers and, indeed, non-readers (like Petrarch).

The Homeric poems have been the object of study for over two and a half millennia. We know, for example, that Athenian boys were made to learn the poems, and explain difficult Homeric words, in the 5th century BCE. In the library of Alexandria, in the 3rd and 2nd centuries BCE, impressive scholars collected earlier texts of Homer, edited them, and wrote extensive commentaries. Summaries of their notes (known as scholia) made their way into the margins of Byzantine manuscripts. From Byzantium, the manuscripts travelled to Italy, as has already emerged, and there the poems were first printed and published. Current research on Homer, including that presented in this book, draws from this long history of scholarship: the scholia, in particular, remain a crucial resource in Homeric studies. And yet, impressive as this learned tradition is, it does not quite explain the significance of Homer through the centuries.

Many people who never studied, or even read, the *Iliad* or the *Odyssey* contributed to ensuring the survival and success of those two poems. Dante, for example, had no access to ancient Greek epic, yet described a meeting with Homer in the first circle of Hell, and inspired Petrarch in his own quest to import and read a copy of the *Iliad*. Derek Walcott, whose epic poem *Omeros* is one of the most significant contemporary engagements with Homer, claims never to have read the *Iliad* or the *Odyssey*. The last chapter in this book focuses on one key episode—Odysseus' descent into the Underworld—and shows how later poets, from Dante to Walcott, saw this descent as a means of reaching into the past, and of conversing with Homer directly, as if with a living poet.

Chapter 1
Looking for Homer

The first extant sources that mention Homer by name date to the 6th century BCE: from them, we can establish that the Greeks considered him an outstanding and ancient poet—but that they knew nothing certain about him. Even the name 'Homer' was disputed: most authors seemed to use it in a straightforward manner, but some insisted that it was only a nickname which meant 'blind', or 'hostage', and referred to a traumatic episode in the poet's life. (The possible meanings of the name 'Homer' are still debated: it is not a standard Greek personal name, but it is not obviously made up either.) The poet's birthplace was another subject of speculation in antiquity. The oldest traditions mentioned various places in Ionia—that is to say, western Turkey and the nearby islands—claiming that Homer hailed from Chios, Smyrne, or Aeolian Cyme. Some accounts also mentioned Athens, Argos, Rhodes, and Salamis. It was always possible to add to those seven traditional birthplaces of Homer: in a game of one-upmanship, some ancient Greek scholars even claimed that Homer was an Egyptian, or an early Roman, on the grounds that the heroic practices he described resembled those of foreign people. Lucian, writing in the 2nd century CE, made fun of this game, claiming that he had actually travelled to the Island of the Blessed, met Homer in person, and established once and for all that he hailed from Babylon.

Just as there was no agreement about Homer's life, so there were doubts about which poems, exactly, he had composed. The authenticity of the *Iliad* was never questioned, but that of the *Odyssey* sometimes was, and a host of other epic poems—now surviving only in fragments and plot summaries—were sometimes attributed to him, as were several *Homeric Hymns* to the gods. In general, it seems that definitions of Homer's *oeuvre* became gradually more narrow in the course of time. In the 6th and early 5th century BCE, Greek authors treated Homer as the author of whole epic sagas, rather than just two specific poems. For example, when the playwright Aeschylus (*c.*525–456 BCE) claimed that his tragedies were 'slices from the banquet of Homer' he must have had in mind a whole cycle of poems concerning the Trojan War, as well as another cycle dealing with Oedipus, his children, and the war they fought over Thebes.

The historian Herodotus (*c.*484–25 BCE) likewise attributed to Homer several poems about the Trojan and the Theban Wars, but began to express doubt about the authenticity of some: for example, he noticed a contradiction between the *Iliad* and the *Cypria* (a cyclic poem about the initial stages of the Trojan War) and suggested that, of the two, only the *Iliad* was truly Homeric. By the 4th century BCE, it was generally assumed that Homer was the author of the *Iliad* and the *Odyssey* alone: Plato, for example, drew exclusively from those two poems when quoting what 'Homer' had said. Aristotle, a generation later, differentiated between those two poems and the cyclic epics on aesthetic grounds: he pointed out that the *Iliad* and the *Odyssey* were much more tightly composed than other early epic poems, and that Homer 'whether from technique or natural genius' made his poems centre around a single action, rather than present a variety of loosely connected episodes, as the other epics did.

In short, knowledge of what Homer composed was not simply an inherited fact, but a matter of debate—even in antiquity. As views about poetry changed, so did definitions of 'Homer'.

The playwright Aeschylus cared about effective theatre: he saw Homer as a vast epic tradition, from which many plays could be drawn. The historian Herodotus was concerned with factual accuracy: he cross-examined different poems that were generally thought to be Homeric, found that the *Cypria* contradicted the *Iliad*, and proceeded to question its authenticity. The philosopher Aristotle theorized about plot, technique, and talent: the *Iliad* and the *Odyssey* were monumental poems organized around a tight and meticulously conceived structure, he observed, and he insisted that they were the work of an exceptional poet.

Still, even after Aristotle pronounced on Homer, questions remained about what exactly he had composed. In the 3rd and 2nd centuries BCE, scholars working in the library of Alexandria applied ever more stringent criteria in order to establish what was truly Homeric. They analysed in detail the diction and grammar of the *Iliad* and the *Odyssey*, and placed a special sign—a long dash called the *obelos*—next to lines or passages whose authenticity they doubted. They also argued extensively about what Homer might or might not have composed, speculating about his 'character' (*ēthos*) and 'persona' (*prosōpon*). Artists working in this period were also interested in character, and attempted to depict the face of Homer with naturalistic realism, on the basis of what was said about him (see Figure 1). Their efforts did not reveal the actual author of the *Iliad* and the *Odyssey*, of course, but testified to a sustained interest in his identity and appearance—an interest that is still in evidence today (see Figure 2). As Pliny observed in his *Natural History*, 'desire gives birth to the image of a face, even when it has not been transmitted, as is the case with Homer'.

Given that the ancient Greeks knew nothing certain about Homer, it is tempting to dismiss their views altogether, and start afresh with an analysis of the poems attributed to him and the contexts of their reception. In fact, however, it would be impossible to begin with a clean slate. We inherited from the Greeks not just

1. **A Roman copy of a Hellenistic portrait of Homer (*c.*150 BCE). Several other ancient portraits survive, testifying to the popularity of Homer as a subject of visual representation.**

the name of Homer—and several portraits and legends about him—but a habit of discussing the *Iliad*, the *Odyssey*, and indeed the cyclic epics in terms of their putative author(s). Epic poems that have been transmitted anonymously do not have the same history of reception or interpretation.

After Petrarch addressed himself to Homer, other scholars went on to learn Greek, produce Latin translations, and interpret the epics. They found the Homeric poems surprising—especially in relation to the fame and reputation of their author. The philosopher Giambattista Vico (1668–1744) was the first to argue that the Homeric epics could not be the creation of a great poet, but rather stemmed from the collective, popular culture of the ancient Greeks. He insisted that they were too 'vile, rude, cruel, proud...unreasonable, frivolous and light' to be the product of a

7

2. 'Photographically realistic painting of Homer' (2013). This work, by South Korean artist C. J. Joongwon, went viral on the Internet, partly because it fuelled speculation about what it might mean to claim 'realism' in the case of Homer.

great writer, and added that inconsistencies of style and factual detail pointed to collective authorship.

A few decades later, the German scholar Friedrich August Wolf (1759–1824) rigorously formulated the Homeric Question on the basis of the scholia found in an important Byzantine manuscript, the Venetus A, which had recently been published. He concluded that Homeric epic was the product of ancient editing and revision based on early, oral compositions. Wolf's *Prolegomena ad Homerum* (1795) privileged the history of the text over the identification of an original poet: Wolf admired the work of the Alexandrian scholars, as preserved in the scholia, and insisted that modern philologists could do even better. His *Prolegomena* defined classics as a modern discipline, and that is understandable, given how strongly he suggested the possibility of philological progress. And yet even Wolf could not escape the ancient terms of the debate about Homer. This is how Goethe satirized his work in a biting couplet:

Der Wolfische Homer
> Sieben Städte zankten sich drum, ihn geboren zu haben;
> nun da der Wolf ihn zerriß, nehme sich jede ihr Stück.

Wolf's Homer
> Seven cities squabbled over which one gave birth to him;
> now that the Wolf tore him apart, let each have a piece.

Apart from the pun on Wolf's name and the general irreverence, Goethe cast doubt on Wolf's achievement by suggesting that there had always been arguments over the identity of Homer, and that a plurality of authors has always threatened to emerge from them. Himself a poet, Goethe advocated a focus on Homeric poetry, rather than the scholarly controversies surrounding it—but in fact the two could not be kept apart. As Nietzsche pointed out in his inaugural lecture at the University of Basel, in 1869, 'Homer as the poet of the *Iliad* and the *Odyssey* is not a transmitted, historical fact—but rather an aesthetic judgement'.

Wolf's *Prolegomena* inspired the work of later scholars called Analysts, who sought to attribute different parts of the Homeric poems to different authors. Unitarians reacted by insisting on the artistic integrity of the poems: they had to be the work of one poet, they argued, even if little could be known about him, since there was a clear unity of composition and intent. In different forms and guises, such arguments endure. To this day, some classicists see the *Iliad* and the *Odyssey* as the work of one exceptional poet, or perhaps two, while others postulate a drawn-out process of composition, and recomposition, in performance. Precisely because there is no overall agreement about the Homeric Question, Chapters 2 and 3 set out what evidence there is concerning the creation of the poems.

Chapter 4 discusses the voice of the poet as it emerges from the poems attributed to him. Chapters 5 to 7 introduce the *Iliad*, while the Chapters 8 to 10 are devoted to the *Odyssey*. Overall, the interpretation offered in this book suggests that Nietzsche was right: arguments about the composition of the *Iliad* and the *Odyssey* are intertwined with judgements about their beauty.

Chapter 2
Textual clues

To modern ears, the *Iliad* and the *Odyssey* sound strangely
repetitive: Achilles is always 'swift-footed', even though for most
of the *Iliad* he refuses to move. Dawn is invariably 'rosy-fingered',
and the sea 'wine-coloured': no variations of hue or atmosphere
are recorded. What are we to make of these set phrases, and what
can they tell us about how the poems were composed? Homeric
formulae, as these phrases are called, are important evidence for
the Homeric Question. The decisive breakthrough concerning
their function was made in the 1930s, when a dashing young
American scholar, Milman Parry, set off to record the oral epics
performed in what was then Yugoslavia. Together with his colleague
Albert Lord, he spent many days and evenings in Bosnian coffee
houses, listening to illiterate epic singers, and recording their
performances (see Figure 3). Through a systematic study of their
techniques, he demonstrated that they relied on a complex
system of formulae which helped them describe characters,
places, actions, and situations to a specific epic rhythm—without
having to take too long thinking over appropriate turns of phrase
in the course of performance. He was also able to show that the
same techniques were used in the composition of Homeric epic.

In the Greek tradition, each epic line is made up of a sequence of
six units, and is therefore called 'the hexameter', literally 'the six
measures'. Each unit (except for the shorter last one) comprises one

3. Milman Parry's assistant Nikola Vujnović, on the left, together with the singer Salih Ugljaninć (1933): their performances, as well as those of other South-Slavic singers, were crucial in reconstructing the techniques used to compose Homeric epic.

long syllable (represented by a dash (—)) and two short syllables (∪∪), which can be replaced by a second long one. Parry showed that, if an epic singer wanted to say 'Achilles', he could choose between different formulae, each of which was designed to take up a different number of measures in the line. Depending on how long he needed to take over it, he could either say 'Achilles', or 'luminous Achilles', or 'swift-footed Achilles', or 'swift-footed luminous Achilles', and thereby reach the end of the line. He would then breathe, organize his thoughts, and embark on the next line of poetry. This was the formulaic system for Achilles, when he was the subject of a sentence:

- ∪∪ | - ∪∪ | - ∪∪ | -∪∪ | - ∪∪ | - ∪

- ∪∪ | - ∪∪ | - ∪∪ | -∪∪ | *dios Achilleus*
　　　　　　　　　　　　luminous Achilles

- ∪∪ | - ∪∪ | - ∪∪ | - *podas okys Achilleus*
　　　　　　　　　　swift-footed Achilles

- ∪∪ | - ∪∪ | - ∪ *podarkes dios Achilleus*
　　　　　　　　swift-footed luminous Achilles

12

Singers chose a formula not because Achilles was, in the particular situation described, luminous rather than swift-footed, but because they needed a formula with a specific metrical shape. Parry demonstrated the principle of 'formulaic economy' for both Homeric and South-Slavic epic: in each tradition, there tended to be one formula that answered to a particular metrical need. If an early Greek singer had two measures to fill, he would always say 'luminous Achilles'—no other formula of that length was available to him. Parry offered many detailed analyses of formulaic systems, showing how different expressions developed in different grammatical cases and covered varying numbers of syllables. He argued that these systems were honed over generations, and provided a means of composing epic swiftly and surely, in front of live audiences.

Milman Parry died young, and it is a great shame that we shall never know what other insights he might have offered, had he been able to carry on with his research. Fortunately, his friend and colleague Albert Lord further developed his comparative approach, arguing that epic singers also made use of larger prefabricated structures, which he called 'themes', following Parry's own terminology, but which are today more often called 'type scenes', which is what Walter Arend (another important scholar of the 1930s) called them.

When epic singers needed to describe episodes of fighting, feasting, sailing, or just about anything else, they followed pre-established patterns, which they could then shorten, expand, and adapt, depending on the immediate needs of the story they were singing, and the audience they needed to please. Thus, for example, a scene of combat between two warriors generally began with a description of each fighter—including background information, and sometimes a simile—followed by an exchange of threats, and the first attack. Or again, when a warrior was about to be killed by his opponent, he sometimes engaged in a final act of supplication—a ritual that featured also in non-martial contexts, and was well-codified in epic. The basic structure of supplication scenes was in three parts: first the suppliant approached, then he or she touched the knees and chin of the person being entreated, and delivered a speech making a request and offering compensation. Descriptions of type scenes, such as the ones I have just given, often sound rigid, but their realization in epic is flexible and sophisticated, as soon emerges when looking at examples. There is, in fact, no 'standard' pattern from which individual examples deviate, but only flexible variations of general structures. Epic singers will have taught each other the building blocks of their art, but what we experience as audiences and readers are nuanced epic tales.

Parry and Lord did not prove that the *Iliad* and the *Odyssey* were 'oral poems' (after all, what we have are written texts), but rather demonstrated that Homeric epic stemmed from a long and sophisticated tradition of oral composition, and recomposition, in performance. What role, if any, the technology of writing played remains an open question. For his part, Lord believed that the *Iliad* and the *Odyssey* were composed right at the moment of transition from orality to writing—when an exceptional epic poet, still entirely versed in oral techniques, realized the potential of writing, and dictated the *Iliad* to a scribe. In short, he imagined that Homer operated in roughly the same way as the singers he and Parry recorded. An exact correspondence of this kind seems, however, unlikely. In general, the problem with using comparative arguments, when tackling the Homeric Question, is deciding how far to push the comparison. South-Slavic singers were responding to assured Harvard-educated scholars with state-of-the-art recording equipment, scholars determined to solve a historical question. They were told to perform for the purposes of recording and transcription, and were moreover asked to compose long epics, in order to match the Homeric prototype. The conditions in early Greece must have been very different.

It is true that the Greek alphabet developed at about the same time as the *Iliad* and the *Odyssey* took shape (see Chapter 3), but it would be surprising if anybody at the time had as clear a vision of the significance of this technology in literary history as Parry and Lord did. It thus seems best to admit that we know very little about how the *Iliad* and the *Odyssey* were composed, and that they are likely to be the result of complicated processes involving both orality and writing, which we can no longer reconstruct in detail.

What we do know is that the techniques of oral composition fundamentally shaped Homeric epic. For this reason, we need to understand how oral techniques worked—not only in order to reconstruct how the poems were composed, but also in order to interpret them. Parry himself was pessimistic about the import of his insights for an aesthetic appreciation of Homeric epic. He argued that formulae had no special meaning in relation to the context in which they were used, that audiences felt 'indifferent' towards them, and that they were perhaps best left untranslated. In short, he treated them as tools of composition—epic blocks of language, which helped singers perform to the rhythm of the hexameter, but which had no further poetic function. Today, this seems very reductive. Formulae are not equivalent to an instrumental interlude, say, or a bit of humming, or some other form of metrical 'filling': they are words, and affect audiences through their meaning, as well as through their rhythmic qualities.

Many formulae are unobtrusive. Characters are often called 'luminous', for example, and several other standard expressions convey a sense of brightness. They have the effect of a general sheen or polish, which makes the epic world gleam. Other formulae define individual characters. Only Achilles, for example, is called 'swift-footed'—and this tells us how he is expected to be and behave, whether or not he lives up to that expectation. The most important stories about him are connected to his swiftness of foot: at the end of the *Iliad*, for example, he chases Hector to his death, in what is one of the most memorable episodes in the whole poem (see Chapter 7). Sometimes, the formula 'swift-footed Achilles' fits the context in which it is used, but more often it creates a dissonance between the way Achilles is described and what he happens to be doing: after all, for most of the *Iliad*, swift-footed Achilles refuses to move. The traditional formulations of epic help to draw attention to how things should be, and measure the distance to how they actually are. For example, when Achilles refuses to enter into battle and chase the enemy, we know that the story has taken a bad turn, and that he is failing to live up to the very formulae that describe him.

One of the ways in which the *Iliad* stands out as a poem of exceptional insight is that it includes reflection on the meaning of its formulaic language. So, for example, when Achilles finally gets up and runs (after Apollo, disguised as a mortal), the god reminds him that there are limitations even to his swiftness of foot:

> 'Son of Peleus, why are you pursuing me on swift feet,
> you a mortal and I an immortal god? You have not even
> recognized me as a god, such is your ceaseless raging.
> …'
> Then swift-footed Achilles, deeply angered, addressed him:
> 'You have thwarted me, Far-Shooter, most deadly of gods
> …
> but I would make you pay for this, if only I had the power.'

The poet elaborates on Achilles' defining formula, and draws attention to his human limitations: Achilles' impotence, futile fury, and imminent death are all captured in this brief exchange between the swift-footed hero and the god Apollo who is faster than him.

There are, to be sure, other, more light-hearted ways in which formulae and type scenes are exploited in Homeric epic. In book 6 of the *Odyssey*, for example, we are confronted with an unprecedented situation, which no traditional 'type scene' can quite capture. Odysseus has just suffered shipwreck, and is now sleeping, naked and exhausted, under some bushes in an

Homer

unknown land. A local princess, Nausicaa, has just finished washing clothes nearby, and is now playing ball with her maids. When the ball falls into the water, the girls shriek, and Odysseus wakes up. He soon realizes that he needs to approach the girls, and ask them for help—indeed, that his life depends on their good will, given how tired and hungry he is. The problem is that, in his current state, he is unlikely to make a good impression. The poet cunningly adapts the structure of the Iliadic battle scene, in order to describe Odysseus' predicament. First, our hero dons an armour (of sorts); then he goes out to face the girls, looking like a raging lion; and finally he addresses a speech to his opponent, the princess Nausicaa:

> Glorious Odysseus came out from under the thicket;
> with his brawny hand he broke off a branch of the dense brushwood,
> a leafy one, to hold before his body and hide his man's private parts.
> He set off like a mountain-nurtured lion, trusting in its strength,
> buffeted by rain and wind as it goes along, and the eyes in it are
> blazing; it is hunting after cattle or sheep, or after
> deer in the wild, and its belly drives it on to make an
> attack on a closely built fold and go after the sheep there.
> Just so Odysseus faced the lovely-haired girls' company,
> naked though he was, because necessity had come upon him.
> And a fearful sight he presented to them, disfigured by brine,
> and they fled in terror, this way and that along the sides of the beach.
> Only the daughter of Alcinous stood unmoved, for Athena
> had put boldness in her heart and taken the fear from her limbs.
> So she stood, holding her ground before him; and Odysseus deliberated
> whether he should grasp the lovely girl by the knees and supplicate her,
> or if he should stand away, just where he was, and entreat her with
> soft words to give him clothing and direct him to the city.

Odysseus moves forward, 'trusting in his strength', a typical image of the Homeric battlefield. Nausicaa, for her part, prepares to 'hold her ground', relying on the 'courage' which Athena inspires. These martial touches express some aspects of the situation: like an Iliadic warrior, Odysseus is in mortal danger, and must turn the encounter to his advantage, if he is to live. But there are other ways in which the traditional battlefield language is incongruous, and even comical: Odysseus, the great warrior, is now ready 'to face the lovely-haired girls', imperfectly covered by a 'leafy branch'.

Odysseus must somehow persuade the young Nausicaa that she has nothing to fear, and that is hard to do when you look like a ravenous lion (see Figure 4). The dramatic flight of the other girls raises the possibility of Odysseus' failure, and leads him to consider supplication as a last resort. In the *Iliad*, defeated warriors supplicate their opponents from a position of utter weakness. Here, Odysseus thinks about supplicating Nausicaa because, on the contrary, he looks strong—and then he worries that touching her knees might further exacerbate the problem. In the end, he decides to adapt the traditional supplication scene to his own purposes: he speaks as a suppliant, but keeps his distance. Just like Odysseus, the poet of the *Odyssey* knows how to use traditional patterns to suit his aim: he depicts a post-Iliadic world, where survival depends on being adaptable—and he adapts traditional battlefield formulations to this new story.

Epic formulae and type scenes do not settle all aspects of the Homeric Question but, because they form the idiom of Homeric epic, they need to be understood in order to interpret the *Iliad* and the *Odyssey*. They are also crucial in order to understand the unusual language in which the poems are composed. Homeric Greek is an artificial and extraordinarily rich mixture of several different dialects: it was never spoken by any real-life community, but rather developed in order to sing the deeds of gods and men to the rhythm of the hexameter. The predominant colouring is Ionic, but there is also a strong Aeolic component. Linguists also identify other influences, including several Attic elements, though these mainly concern matters of spelling, and therefore testify to the influence of a written Athenian text, rather than an early Athenian contribution to epic diction. Students who read the poems in

4. Athenian cup depicting Odysseus and Nausicaa, 5th century BCE. The other side of the cup depicts the encounter between Oedipus and the Sphinx—another situation in which a hero must use his wits in addressing a female interlocutor.

Greek for the first time are often bewildered by the number of ways in which something simple, like 'was' or 'to be', can be expressed, and this was also the reaction in antiquity, when scholars claimed that Homer knew 'all dialects'. Some forms seem relatively recent, and others are very old. There may even be remnants of Mycenaean Greek, which was spoken in the second millennium BCE. All these forms seem, on the whole, to serve a familiar purpose: they provide metrically useful alternatives for composing poetry to the rhythm of the hexameter. They exist, that is, as part of a well-developed formulaic system.

Homeric Greek confirms the existence of a long tradition of epic composition in performance, but also offers more specific clues about where and when the Homeric poems took shape. The dominant Ionic colouring and irreducible traces of Aeolic point precisely to the area where, in ancient legend, Homer was supposed to have lived—the coast of western Turkey and the neighbouring Greek islands. Other tiny details in the poems seem to confirm this: for example, in an unobtrusive simile, the poet mentions a specific river in western Turkey, as if he expected his audience to be familiar with the vast and varied flocks of birds that gathered by its banks. Knowledge of other areas of Greece seems more hazy, as I argue in Chapter 3.

Linguistic analysis also helps to date the *Iliad* and the *Odyssey*, at least in relation to the other poems that were attributed to Homer in antiquity. It seems that these two epics were not only the longest and most admired but, in linguistic terms, the most ancient. Other poems show a greater incidence of recent forms, suggesting that they were composed later, or remained in a fluid state which admitted linguistic change and innovation for longer than the *Iliad* and the *Odyssey*. The trouble with arguments based on language, however, is that they do not yield absolute dates. We can reconstruct a sequence of linguistic changes (i.e. which forms are older, which younger, and hence which poems sound more archaic) but not when those changes took place. In order to investigate when the *Iliad* and *Odyssey* were composed in absolute terms, it is necessary therefore to consider archaeological evidence.

Chapter 3
Material clues

The father of Homeric archaeology was a flamboyant character, with only tenuous links to the academic establishment. At a time when professional Analysts were dissecting the Homeric poems in a quest to identify different authors and layers of composition, Heinrich Schliemann (1822–90) set out to prove the historical reality of Troy. The son of a protestant minister, Schliemann had received some classical training in his early youth but, when his father was caught embezzling church funds, he had to leave formal education and make a living for himself—as an apprentice to a grocer, a cabin boy, a book keeper, and an import/export agent in Russia. It was in this latter capacity that he started to amass what would eventually become a very considerable capital.

After joining the gold rush in California for a few months (until a Rothschild agent complained about short-weight consignments), and working as a military contractor during the Crimean War, he was finally in a position to devote himself to an ambition which, as he later claimed, he had harboured since childhood: discovering ancient Troy, and proving it was a real city. Surprisingly, this is precisely what he managed to do: he excavated at the site of modern Hisarlık in Turkey, and discovered an impressive fortified citadel. He hacked away through several different archaeological layers, until he got to the bottom, and discovered treasure. A picture of

MME. SCHLIEMANN, IN THE PARURE OF HELEN OF TROY

5. **Sophia Schliemann wearing treasures discovered by her husband at the site of ancient Troy, *c.*1874.**

his young Greek wife, donning ancient jewellery, became a symbol of his expedition, and electrified the public (see Figure 5).

The response of professional classicists was distinctly cooler. Ulrich von Wilamowitz-Moellendorff, the most influential philologist of his time, delivered his verdict in 1906:

> Heinrich Schliemann rummaged through the ground of the Greek city of Ilium, unencumbered by any linguistic or historical scholarship, driven on by the naïve belief that anything which is in Homer must be real…It was understandable that the world should applaud his discoveries; and at least excusable that the masses, who cannot grasp historical scholarship, should take the real treasures as proof of the reality of the Homeric account… One does not inveigh against this sort of thing; but one does not take it seriously either.

Schliemann insisted that discovering Troy had been his childhood ambition—and Wilamowitz proposed to treat his work very precisely as child's play. In fact, Schliemann made a decisive contribution to Homeric scholarship, even if the relationship between poetry and archaeology was more complex than he allowed.

The ruins at Hisarlık, together with further excavations at Mycenae and Tiryns in mainland Greece (which Schliemann also directed), prove that impressive civilizations flourished in the second millennium BCE—and in some of the same locations that featured prominently in Homeric epic. Linear B tablets found at Mycenae, Pylos, and other second-millennium sites prove, moreover, that the technology of writing was known in that period. In the 12th century BCE, this Mycenaean civilization suddenly collapsed (for reasons that are still unclear), and a long period of decline ensued, generally known as the Greek 'Dark Ages'. It was only in the 8th century BCE that people living in Greece began to flourish again: the next two centuries saw a sharp increase in the population, the rise of the city-state (*polis*), the construction of the first temples and cult statues of the gods, an upsurge in travel and trade, the foundation of new colonies, and the reintroduction of writing from the Levant (knowledge of Linear B was lost during the Dark Ages).

The question is where Homeric poetry falls in relation to these major historical developments. When Michael Ventris and John Chadwick deciphered Linear B in the 1950s, classicists hoped to recover early versions of Homeric poetry—or at least stories of gods and men expressed in the hexameter rhythm. However, Mycenaean tablets yielded nothing of the sort. On the evidence of what survives, it seems that Linear B was used exclusively to record matter-of-fact lists and inventories. Still, even these bureaucratic Bronze Age documents did perhaps suggest some connections with Homeric epic. Tablets from Pylos show, for example, that the cult of Poseidon was especially important there, and the *Odyssey* conveys the same impression.

Even if some traces of Mycenaean language and culture may perhaps be detected, the *Iliad* and the *Odyssey* were certainly composed after the Dark Ages. They refer to material circumstances not found before the later 8th or early 7th century BCE, such as temples and cult statues, narrative art, and knowledge of the world extending from Thrace to Phoenicia and Egypt. This gives a *terminus post quem*: the poems cannot have been composed much before 700 BCE. What complicates the picture is that they are set in a much earlier age.

From the point of view of even the earliest Homeric audiences, the Trojan War belonged to the remote past, and the heroes who fought there seemed, in some ways, like a separate race altogether: stronger, closer to the gods but also, in some ways, more primitive, prone to extreme emotions, and lacking in social cohesion. Greek communities of the archaic period worshipped the heroes, sacrificed at their tombs, and hoped for their help and protection. In fact, hero cult and epic poetry developed in parallel in the 8th and 7th centuries BCE: worship at impressive ancient burial sites went together with a flourish of stories about those who fought at Troy.

In the *Iliad* we are told that the heroes could easily throw boulders 'that no two men could lift, such as they are nowadays'. Their diet (a topic that fascinated ancient Homeric scholars) also marked them out as different: the heroes seemed to feed almost exclusively on meat, whereas the diet of real-life Greek communities consisted mostly of pulses, fruit, and vegetables. Agriculture provided what people ate on a daily basis; red meat was primarily consumed at religious festivals, when large animals were sacrificed and then eaten immediately, before the food could spoil. In short, the heroes ate every day what Homeric audiences savoured only on ritual occasions.

Homeric similes also express subtle differences between the world of the heroes and that familiar to the poet and his audiences.

Thus, for example, Ajax withdraws slowly and unwillingly from the battlefield, like a donkey driven away from a cornfield by the blows of children; Athena diverts an arrow that is about to hit Menelaus 'as a mother who brushes away a fly from her sleeping baby'; and Odysseus wears a tunic whose material is as thin and shiny as the skin of an onion. The world of the similes often seems more humble than that described in the main narrative—but also technologically more advanced.

Fishing is a case in point, just to keep to the subject of diet. In the *Iliad* nobody eats fish, in the *Odyssey* it is consumed only once—as a last resort in order to avoid starvation. Several similes, however, reveal not only that fishing was a routine activity in the world of the poet, but also that it involved sophisticated technology and skill. In fact, the similes often describe technical matters: how a roof is made with interlocking beams, how silver is overlaid with gold, how an ivory mouthpiece is stained with purple. The comparisons made in the poems reveal a keen interest in the skill of ordinary men and women. The heroes, by contrast, often resemble forces of nature, and wild animals—lions and boars that threaten organized human farming, for example. There is, then, a sense that the heroes are stronger than ordinary people, but also that they would not have the patience or the peace required to engage in the many technical activities portrayed in the similes with palpable admiration.

Some Homeric passages comment explicitly on how things have changed since the time when the heroes fought at Troy. At the beginning of *Iliad* 12, for example, the poet insists that no trace remains of a wall that the 'Achaeans' (i.e. the Greek contingent) built around their camp. In that passage, he even calls the warriors who died at Troy 'a race of demi-god men', drawing attention to their superhuman status. Later in the *Iliad*, there is a brief allusion to the hero cult that awaits Sarpedon, mortal son of Zeus, once he is dead and buried in Lycia. There are other vague allusions to hero worship in the poems, but they are rare—and this seems surprising at first, given how prominent hero cult was in archaic Greece. It seems that Homeric epic, rather than emphasizing the great posthumous honours accorded to the heroes, dramatizes how hard they themselves found the prospect of dying.

Ruins represented the most tangible connection between the world of the heroes and that of Homeric audiences. Impressive fortifications at Troy, Mycenae, and other second-millennium sites could clearly be seen in the 8th and 7th centuries BCE, and testified to a grander age, a past civilization when men were, indeed, able to handle massive boulders. It cannot be coincidence that Troy, in particular, was situated very near the places traditionally associated with Homer's birth, and where we know epic diction developed: the ruins there must have inspired grand poetry (see Figure 6).

The *Iliad* and the *Odyssey* describe a distant, mythical past—even from the point of view of their earliest audiences—but are set in a

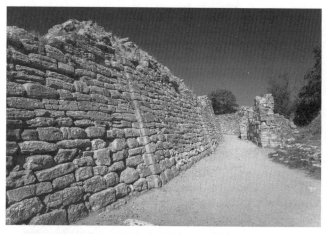

6. The Walls of Troy, *c.*1200 BCE. At the time when the *Iliad* was composed, *c.*700 BCE, these impressive ruins spoke of an earlier and grander age.

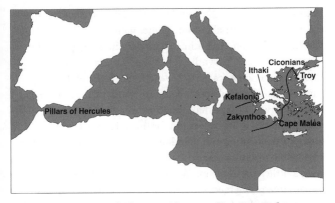

7. Map of the journey of Odysseus. After rounding Cape Malea,
Odysseus' journey can no longer be traced on a map. Readers,
however, have always been keen to establish his exact itinerary.
The Romans insisted that he travelled to Italy. Dante later told the
story of how, in a second and final journey, he sailed past the Pillars
of Hercules (see Chapter 10).

real and recognizable landscape. This does not mean that all
Homeric locations can be securely placed on a map. A portion of
Odysseus' journey home, from when he is blown off course at Cape
Malea until he wakes up in Ithaca, cannot easily be traced (see
Figure 7), although many ancient and modern readers have tried
to do so. The Romans, in particular, insisted that he had reached
Sicily and mainland Italy. It is no coincidence that, precisely
during this part of his journey, Odysseus meets the most unlikely
characters: the god Aeolus in his castle full of winds; the one-eyed
giant Polyphemus; the dangerous Circe, who turns his companions
into pigs; the shades of the dead in the murky Underworld; the
Sirens; Scylla and Charybdis; Calypso; and the Phaeacians, who
finally offer to take him home on one of their magical ships, which
'steer a course by their own intelligence and never suffer shipwreck'.

The case of Ithaca is different: this was clearly meant to be a real
place, an island off the western coast of Greece, but the Homeric
description does not quite match realities on the ground.

According to Homer, Ithaca is 'farthest of all the islands towards the west', modern Ithaki is not. Homer names four islands (Same, Ithaca, Doulichion, Zacynthus), a modern map suggests three (Kefalonia, Ithaki, Zakynthos). Scholars have tried hard to line up Homeric Ithaca with the actual geography of the area, suggesting for example that Odysseus' island might be modern Kefalonia rather than Ithaki, and further invoking massive earthquakes in order to account for the differences between Homeric description and local landscape. But perhaps it is more reasonable to assume that the exact contours of western Greece were a little hazy in the mind of early epic audiences. After all, as has already emerged, Homeric poetry originated in Ionia, hundreds of miles further east. It is also clear that the needs of the narrative, and the formulations and reformulations of epic, partly shaped Homeric landscapes (it is possible for example that an adjective was reinterpreted as a place name, and other evolutions of this kind).

Similar considerations to those concerning Homeric landscape also apply to Homeric society: no real-life community ever lived like the people described in epic poetry. The *Iliad* and the *Odyssey* reveal how the Greeks of the archaic period imagined the great heroes of the past. Those heroes were much stronger than 'men such as they are nowadays', but also more quarrelsome and selfish. As the opening of the *Iliad* makes clear, when Achilles falls out with Agamemnon, leader of the expedition against Troy, over possession of a slave girl, he decides to prove his worth by inflicting countless agonies upon the Achaeans—that is to say, the Greek warriors on whose side he is supposed to be fighting. Odysseus manages to save not one of the men who fought under his command at Troy, and when he finally gets home, he seems determined to start a civil war. Historians point out that in the early first millennium BCE, authority was diffuse, and clashes between leaders must have been common. It is also true, however, that the rapid social and political changes of the 7th century—when we can trace expanding communities, new settlements, increased trade and travel—provide an appropriate context for poetic explorations of authority.

The main point, here, is that no interpretation leads to a single original audience, or historical context, or specific political agenda in support of which the Homeric poems must have been composed. Flawed leaders like Agamemnon are always interesting, as are critics of authority like Achilles. As for Odysseus, the consummate survivor, he has navigated the human mind for almost three millennia. In short, the *Iliad* and the *Odyssey* tell stories of broad appeal, and this makes it difficult to determine exactly why and for whom they were originally composed.

Because the poems are set in the distant past, descriptions of epic performances found in them cannot be used as straightforward evidence for how the Homeric poems themselves were composed and delivered. The *Odyssey* depicts two professional singers: the blind bard Demodocus, who entertains Odysseus at the court of the Phaeacians, and Phemius, who sings for the pleasure of the suitors in Ithaca. Their repertoire is linked to the events and themes explored in the *Iliad* and the *Odyssey* themselves: Demodocus tells the story of a quarrel between Achilles and Odysseus, then of the love affair between Ares and Aphrodite, and finally (at Odysseus' request) of the Trojan Horse, the great ruse Odysseus himself devised in order to win the war. Phemius sings of the Achaeans' return journeys from Troy—a topic that pains Penelope, because her own husband is still missing, but is acceptable to Telemachus because, he claims, 'people praise the newest songs'. It seems then that epic performances in the *Odyssey* are extemporaneous affairs, sung over dinner. They probably reflect the early origins of epic (occasional entertainment at aristocratic gatherings) but do not offer specific clues about how or why the Homeric poems themselves were composed.

The *Iliad* is more than 15,000 lines long, and must have taken approximately three full days (or nights) to perform from start to finish. The *Odyssey* is almost as long. These monumental epics must have been intended for reperformance—they certainly did not rely on people who always praised 'the newest song', because the effort required to compose, perform, and indeed receive them was not justifiable in terms of a one-off experience. In short, the poems required commitment and organization. Some form of institutional support must have been necessary, in order to establish breaks, ensure adequate food supplies, and arrange for other facilities during a long period of recitation.

Just as there are differences between the occasional performances described in the *Odyssey* and the monumental epics attributed to Homer, so the technology of writing must have featured more prominently in the age when the poems were composed than in the age they were meant to describe. There is only one reference to writing, or something close to it, in Homeric epic. The *Iliad* tells the story of the handsome Bellerophontes, who rejected the attentions of a married woman when she tried to seduce him. Enraged and humiliated, the woman then complained to her husband that Bellerophontes had tried to make love to her, and demanded that he be put to death:

> …anger seized her lord at what he had heard,
> but he held back from killing, for he felt awe at this in his heart;
> instead he sent Bellerophontes to Lycia, and gave him deadly signs,
> many life-destroying things, marked by him in a folded tablet,
> and told him to show these to his host in Lycia, so ensuring his death.

Whatever these signs were (perhaps a script, perhaps an ad hoc code, or some kind of drawing), they amounted to nothing good. Bellerophontes managed to avoid being killed in Lycia, but his attempted murder by writing did not represent proper heroic behaviour. In the *Iliad*, writing is presented as a devious trick, but ideas about what was appropriate in the heroic age did not necessarily apply to the age when the poems took shape.

The technology of writing must at some point have been used (otherwise we would not now have the poems). After the Dark Ages, in the second half of the 8th century BCE, Greek communities adopted an alphabetic script based on West Semitic writing. A modest clay cup found in Ischia, an island off the coast of Naples, offers important evidence for Homeric epic (see Figure 8). An inscription of some lines of poetry, scratched on its side, and dating to about 740–720 BCE, proudly announces: 'I am the cup of Nestor…'

In the *Iliad*, Nestor is the owner of an amazing cup, made of solid gold, which he alone is strong enough to lift (a puzzling detail to ancient as well as modern readers, given that Nestor is old in the *Iliad*, and not the strongest of the Achaeans). There is no physical resemblance between the modest clay vessel found on Ischia and Nestor's famous cup in the *Iliad*, but the inscription may well be a playful reference to the poem, or some other epic tale about the legendary Nestor and his cup. The extremely regular layout of the verse inscription may reflect the influence of epic texts written on papyrus or leather, though such texts (if they existed) need not have been our *Iliad* or *Odyssey*. Some scholars have speculated that writing was introduced in Greece precisely for the purpose of recording Homeric epic—but there is no way of proving anything of the sort. Indeed, the suggestion seems unlikely (the West Semitic script had obvious practical applications, for trade for example), and the cup from Ischia may well predate our poems.

Even at a time when texts of the *Iliad* and the *Odyssey* must have existed, all we hear about are oral recitations. We know that, in the 6th century BCE, the tyrant Pisistratus or one of his sons passed a decree, according to which the Homeric poems had to be recited in their entirety and in the correct order at the most important city festival, the Great Panathenaea. Scripts must have existed by then, and facilitated the task. By *c.*520 BCE we also know that Theagenes of Rhegium, in southern Italy, was writing about Homer: if there were texts about Homer, it makes sense to assume

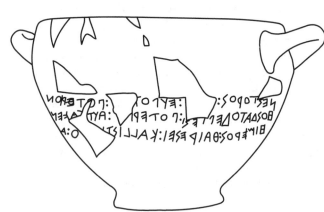

8. 'Nestor's Cup' with line drawing of its inscription (*c.*740–720 BCE). This drinking cup found on the island of Ischia, near Naples, bears one of the earliest inscriptions in the alphabetic Greek script. The text may allude to the famous cup of Nestor, which also features in the *Iliad*.

there were also texts of his poems. Still, the emphasis of our sources remains on performance rather than writing: what grabbed the attention of the Greeks was the work of professional entertainers called rhapsodes, who recited the Homeric epics at the Panathenaea and many other city festivals around the Greek-speaking world. Material evidence confirms that, by the late archaic period, knowledge of the poems was widespread. Greek vases, found in many different locations, display paintings inspired specifically by the *Iliad* and the *Odyssey*, as opposed to more generalized epic themes. Together with the earliest extant quotations from, and references to, Homer in the work of other poets, they provide a *terminus ante quem* for the *Iliad* and the *Odyssey*: by the late 6th century BCE, the poems were well-known throughout the Greek world.

Chapter 4
The poet in the poems

As has already emerged, we have little evidence about the person or people responsible for the composition of the *Iliad* and the *Odyssey*. Within the epics themselves, however, the voice of the narrator can clearly be heard. That voice was important to ancient audiences and readers, influencing what they thought about the legendary 'Homer'—and that voice remains important today, not because it reveals the actual author(s) of the poems, but because it characterizes the narrative.

The *Iliad* starts with an order—'Sing, goddess, the wrath of Achilles'—and the goddess evidently complies with this command, because what we then hear is precisely a song about Achilles' wrath. After the opening invocation, the poet and the Muse sing in unison: it is no longer possible to distinguish the poet's voice from that of the goddess. At times of exceptional stress, however, the poet seems to lose contact with his divinity, and again we hear him ask for help. Already in book 2, before launching into a lengthy 'Catalogue of Ships', the poet pauses, and reflects on the enormity of what he now needs to deliver, a list of all the Greek leaders and their contingents:

> Tell me now, you Muses who have your homes on Olympus—
> for you are goddesses, are present, and know all things,
> but we have heard only the rumour, and know nothing—
> who were the chief men and lords of the Danaans.

Here the poet draws a clear line between gods and mortals: the Muses ('you') are always present and know everything, whereas the poet and his audience ('we') can at best hear something, but have no certain knowledge. The word that I have translated as 'rumour', in order to preserve its aural quality and its precarious claim to truth, is *kleos*, literally 'that which is heard', but also 'fame', and sometimes specifically 'epic poetry'. In contrast to what is heard, the verb 'to know', in Greek, shares its root with the verb 'to see'. This invocation thus sets divinity, presence, sight, and knowledge above mortality, distance, hearing, and ignorance. What seems surprising, at this point in the narrative, is that the poet sides with his audience, and asks to listen to the Muses. Soon, however, he switches sides, and stands with the Muses, revealing what he sees—and that, as I discuss on pp. 48f., is an extraordinary panorama.

The *Odyssey* also begins with an order: 'Tell me, Muse, of the man of many turns, who wandered far and wide, after he had sacked the sacred city of Troy.' But then the poet expands a little, in order to pass judgement on the morality of Odysseus: he lost all his men before returning to his homeland, but it was not his fault, we are told, since his foolish companions ate the cattle of the Sun, and were punished as a result. Ancient readers worried about this statement, as the scholia testify: 'Here is a problem. Why did the poet speak only of the one ship that the Sun destroyed?' This is, indeed, a good question, since the crew of only one ship ate the cattle of the Sun, and suffered shipwreck as a result. Odysseus lost most of his companions in other circumstances—circumstances for which they were not always to blame.

As well as defending his main character, the poet offers some explicit reflections on his art, and its relationship to power. At the beginning of the *Odyssey*, Telemachus rebukes his mother, because she tries to influence the repertoire of Phemius, the singer who performs in her house. Later, when Odysseus visits the Phaeacians, he praises the local bard Demodocus for his objective account of what happened at Troy: according to Odysseus, he sings 'as if he had been there himself'. Demodocus is blind and does not recognize Odysseus, one of the protagonists of his tale. Precisely for this reason, his account is guaranteed to be objective and truthful, without ulterior motive. (Odysseus rewards Demodocus with a succulent joint of pork, but the singer did not adapt his song in order to please him.) Ancient readers thought that Demodocus was an autobiographical figure, and that Homer himself was blind. They considered that the following lines applied just as well to Homer as to the Phaeacian bard:

> The Muse loved him greatly, and gave him a good gift and a bad:
> she deprived him of his eyes, but gave him sweet song.

The gift of poetry is presented as great but fragile in the *Odyssey*. At the end of the poem, when Odysseus exacts his revenge on the suitors and those who consorted with them, the singer Phemius fears for his life. He begs to be spared, arguing that he has a divine gift for poetry, that he sang for the suitors under duress, and that he will now sing for Odysseus 'as if for a god', if only his life is spared. The first *Odyssey*, the first 'poem about Odysseus', is the result of Odysseus' mercy on the singer.

Already these brief remarks suggest that two rather different narrative voices emerge from the *Iliad* and the *Odyssey*. In the poem about Troy, we are presented with a clear and objective account. In the *Odyssey*, by contrast, the perspective of the poet and that of Odysseus are entangled, also because Odysseus himself takes over the narrative in books 9–12 and is said to sing of his past exploits 'like a bard'. An ancient critic known as 'Longinus' argued that the *Iliad*, with its intense and uncompromising vision, was the work of a poet in his prime, 'the sun at noon', whereas the *Odyssey* was the more speculative, quizzical, and ambiguous work of old age: a sunset. There was less heat in that poem, according to Longinus, more shadow, and 'the tendency of the old to lean towards the fabulous'. Leaving aside biographical speculation about Homer, the narrative voices clearly reflect the different ages and personalities of the main characters.

If we ask from what vantage point the story is told, there seems again to be a difference between the *Iliad* and the *Odyssey*. In the *Iliad*, the position of the narrator in relation to the events he tells can be pinpointed with surprising accuracy. When the poet says 'on the left' or 'on the right', for example, he always looks at the action on the battlefield from the same vantage point: he keeps his back to the sea, facing the plain and the city of Troy beyond it. The curved coastline, with its beached Achaean ships, is arranged before him 'like a theatre', as an ancient scholar put it. When the poet speaks in his own voice, 'left' and 'right' always indicate that he is viewing the action from that position. By contrast, when a Trojan character speaks, 'right' and 'left' are reversed. Although some scholars insist on the poet's even-handed treatment of Trojans and Achaeans in the poem, it follows that he quite literally views the war from the Achaeans' side. His position anchors the narrative and makes it possible for him, and indeed for us, to gain a clear picture of how the action unfolds. A computer simulation of how Iliadic warriors move on the battlefield, based on precise indications given in the text, is now available—and demonstrates the poet's visual control of the action.

As well as describing the fighting from his usual vantage point, hovering somewhere above the Aegean sea and facing Troy, the poet can zoom in and describe tiny details—how a spear breaks through a forehead, for example, making pulp of the brain. He can show how two horses stumble on a branch, and then pan out again, to reveal the whole battlefield in disarray. Contemporary readers often comment on the cinematic qualities of Homeric epic; but, in antiquity, there were no helicopters, no cameras, no medical probes that could enter into wounds and reveal the devastation inside. To ancient audiences, the poet's powers of vision were truly divine.

There are two set pieces, in the *Iliad*, that spectacularly display the poet's ability to survey the landscape, as if from above, and to zoom in and highlight details of microscopic proportions: the 'Catalogue of Ships' in book 2 and the 'Shield of Achilles' in book 18. As has already emerged, at the beginning of the catalogue the poet asks the Muses for help. He then goes on to name the commanders of all the contingents that formed the Trojan expedition, arranging his catalogue spatially, on the basis of the commanders' place of origin (see Figure 9).

He begins in Aulis, where the Achaean fleet gathered before sailing off to Troy, and moves in a spiral around that starting point—in order to name the contingents that gathered from nearby locations (arrow A on the map). A second spiral starts in Lacedaemon—place of origin of the war, since Helen was

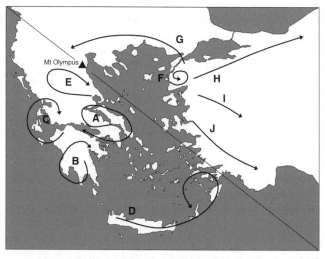

9. **Map of the 'Catalogue of Ships' and the 'Catalogue of the Trojans', in the second book of the *Iliad*. They give a good impression of the poet's panoramic view of the eastern Mediterranean.**

abducted from there (B). A third movement brings the catalogue to Elis, in western Greece, where the poet draws another route, to include Ithaca and Calydon (C). In a fourth spiral, the poet lists the Aegean contingents (D), and then moves to Phthia, Achilles' place of origin, and names nearby contingents in a final spiral (E).

This huge 'Catalogue of Ships' thus concludes with Achilles, his former contribution, and current absence: without him, the Achaeans cannot succeed, however great their fleet. A similar visual control of the landscape emerges from the shorter 'Catalogue of the Trojans', which follows, and lists their allies (arrows F–J on the map). In the absence of Google Earth, we must wonder how the poet could see what he describes. It is perhaps significant that Olympus, vantage point of the gods, lies precisely on the dividing line between Achaean and Trojan contingents: the gods must have had the same commanding view of the landscape as the poet himself.

The description of the 'Shield of Achilles' offers a different example of how the poet sees the world, but likewise reveals his divine powers of vision. When Patroclus returns to the battlefield, Achilles lends him his armour, and thus ends up losing it when his friend is killed and stripped. To help her son when he in turn decides to join the fighting, Thetis asks the god Hephaestus to make new weapons for him. The god sets to work, and the poet shows us what he makes.

The details of Hephaestus' (and the poet's) creation have been much debated, but the overall design seems clear: the shield is round, and features several concentric, decorated bands. Real-life objects, such as Phoenician and Cypriot silver bowls of the 8th and 7th centuries BCE, may have inspired the design, but the shield of Achilles is a divine artefact: stars rise and set at its centre, marking the passing of time in the cosmos; in a different scene, people shout at each other in a court case, and are then pacified by a verdict; in another, warriors organize an ambush, engage in a skirmish, then carry away the dead; elsewhere agricultural work follows the seasons; while, in yet another scene, dancers stamp their feet to the sound of music; and, finally, the river Oceanus flows all around the rim of the shield. It seems that, on this object, images turn into stories.

Perhaps we ought to imagine film strips projected onto each circling section of the shield, complete with sound effects—for this is not silent cinema, but rather an impossible, multimedia, moving and buzzing device. If we consider the size of the shield, the whole creation becomes even more bewildering. At one level, its dimensions are determined by the size of Achilles' body—but the scenes on it are so numerous and detailed that, in order to fit, they would need to be scaled down to microscopic proportions. The poet concentrates the whole world on to the shield of Achilles.

The fact that scenes of peace, as well as war, are included may seem strange—other Homeric shields are designed to frighten the enemy—but here we must distinguish between the poet's ability to see and describe this divine object, and the perspective of characters inside his story. Achilles admires the shield and recognizes, in its stunning intricacy, the work of a divine craftsman; but when his soldiers see it, they cannot endure to look at the contraption, and run away in terror.

Ancient audiences understood that the poet's ability to see and describe the shield was linked to his divine gift for poetry. One ancient biography, for example, gives the following account of Homer's blindness:

> When the poet arrived at the tomb of Achilles, he prayed to behold the hero as he appeared when he went off to battle adorned with the second set of armour. But when he saw Achilles, Homer was blinded by the brightness of the armour. Pitied by Thetis and the Muses, he was honoured by them with the gift of poetry.

As in several other ancient legends, blindness and poetic vision go together: the poet can describe for us an object that, in the *Iliad*, ordinary mortals cannot bear to observe in detail.

In the *Odyssey*, the narrative voice seems closer to Odysseus than to a divine vision of the world. The poet asks the Muse to 'begin from somewhere' in recounting the story of 'the man of many turns'; but, after that initial invocation, he never again asks for divine help. Indeed, immediately after the proem, Zeus complains about mortals who always blame the gods for their own actions. In line with Zeus' programmatic statement, the rest of the *Odyssey* focuses largely on what happens on earth: the gods feature in their interactions with mortals, but scenes set on Olympus are rare. Just as the poet says little about what happens in the divine sphere, so he never offers a panoramic overview of the space within which the narrative unfolds on earth. But for one exception (when Poseidon, travelling back to Olympus from Aethiopia, spots Odysseus on his raft), the story seems to travel in the wake of Odysseus, and thus present the action from sea level. There is even a suggestion that Odysseus will, one day, travel beyond the reach of epic poetry.

When he visits the land of the dead, in book 11, the seer Tiresias predicts that Odysseus will suffer greatly at sea, because the god Poseidon wants to punish him for blinding his son Polyphemus, that he will one day get home, but only after having lost all his men, and that he will then have to embark on a new journey, in order to reach people who do not know about the sea. Once there, he should make a sacrifice to Poseidon as soon as he hears someone mistake his oar for a winnowing fan. There is no indication of where in the world such a mistake could take place, but one thing seems clear: the place where Odysseus must worship Poseidon lies beyond the reach of Homeric epic. Anyone familiar with the *Iliad*, and its massive 'Catalogue of Ships', or the *Odyssey's* account of travel across the wine-dark sea, must know about oars. The poem thus expands beyond the known world not only by imagining mythical lands populated by nymphs and monsters, but also by suggesting that there are some places so far removed from the world of the Greeks that local people know nothing about the sea, and have therefore never heard the great epic poems about the Trojan War and its aftermath.

Although the geographic contours of the *Odyssey* remain vague, in the main narrative the poet tracks Odysseus' movements with great precision. This is particularly obvious in the second half of the poem, when he arrives in Ithaca and prepares his revenge. As soon as Odysseus wakes up in Ithaca, he carefully hides the gifts the Phaeacians gave him in a cave near the beach, and then takes a steep path up the mountains, to the hut of the swineherd Eumaeus. There he tells the swineherd a few lies, gathers crucial intelligence, meets Telemachus, and, disguised as a beggar, makes his way down to the palace. The old dog Argos, 'lying on a pile of manure by the front gates', recognizes him, wags his tail, and then conveniently dies—so that his presence is not revealed by rapturous expressions of canine love. Odysseus now prepares the ground for his attack on the suitors. He tells Telemachus to remove all weapons from the hall, and store them in an inner room; the nurse Eurycleia, meanwhile, should keep the maids busy in yet a different set of rooms, so that they do not notice the transfer of weapons. As the suitors enjoy what will be their last rowdy meal in the hall, Odysseus positions himself by the door: they hardly notice the beggar, but the poet makes sure that we know exactly where he is.

Penelope suddenly makes an entrance, climbing down the stairs with Odysseus' old bow in her hands, and standing 'by a pillar, a support for the roof'. She proposes a contest: whoever manages to string the bow, and shoot an arrow through the rings of twelve axes set in a row, will be her husband. Telemachus declares that he too will take part, and in case of victory will look after his mother himself. The contest begins. Telemachus tries to string the bow three times and, on the third, is about to succeed: Odysseus, however, signals to him to let go, while remaining unobtrusively in his corner. The suitors attempt the challenge themselves, each in turn, starting from those sitting to the right of Antinous, their leader. Throughout the narrative, the poet pays special attention to where exactly the bow ends up, after each contestant attempts to string it, and what the suitors do to it to try and make it bend. We can almost feel Odysseus' eyes fixed on his old bow.

Again without attracting the suitors' attention, Odysseus signals to the swineherd Eumaeus and the herdsman Philoetius to follow him outside. He reveals his identity, and details his plans. They file back into the hall one by one, unobtrusively, and position themselves as told. Eumaeus ensures that the bow ends up in Odysseus' hands, Philoetius locks the hall; Telemachus sends Penelope upstairs into her room. Odysseus now takes the bow, strings it easily, and shoots his arrow through the twelve rings. And then he continues shooting—at the suitors, now. *Odyssey* 22 opens with his initial attack, when he sheds his beggar's rags, leaps on to the threshold of the great hall, and takes aim. (We learn from Plato that this was a favourite scene in the repertoire of epic performers.)

The poet's technique, in describing the lead-up to the death of the suitors, is cinematic, as indeed it often is in the *Iliad*. But the angle is different. Rather than offering an aerial view of the battlefield, and then zooming in and out of the action, here the 'camera' is placed at eye level. We follow the gaze of different characters, as they intercept private signals, or fail to realize what is going on. Odysseus and his accomplices carefully position themselves around the room, and turn their gaze on each other, slowly, silently—while the rowdy suitors brag, sweat, and swagger in the centre. To use a term borrowed from narratology, what we have here is a prime example of 'focalization'—the poet makes us perceive the scene through the eyes of specific characters: Telemachus checking with his father whether it is all right to string the bow; Philoetius stealthily locking the doors under the eyes of his accomplices; Odysseus keeping his gaze fixed on the bow as it passes from suitor to suitor.

When the weapon finally ends up in his hands, after all that build-up, there is a danger that the narrative tension might slacken as he strings the bow. The poet needs to suggest the rapidity and ease with which Odysseus handles his old weapon, and shoots his first arrow; yet he must not let a quick and easy movement turn into a narrative let-down. So he presents Odysseus' action in slow motion, by inserting a simile right in the middle of his description:

> Once he had taken up the great bow and looked it all over,
> as when a man, who well understands the lyre and singing,
> easily, holding it on either side, pulls the strongly twisted
> cord of sheep's gut, so as to slip it over a new peg,
> so, without any strain, Odysseus strung the great bow.
> Then plucking it in his right hand he tested the bowstring,
> and it gave him back an excellent sound, like the voice of a swallow.

Odysseus' achievement and the poet's art are one and the same thing. The audience hear the singer pluck his string, and at the same time see Odysseus test his bow. By glorifying Odysseus' mastery at this crucial point in the story, the poet also aggrandizes himself: as often, in the *Odyssey*, the main character and the singer of tales are brought close together. What is special about the simile, however, is the way in which the performance context and the action in the narrative are superimposed. The poet sings the tale of Odysseus to the accompaniment of his lyre, and at the same time Odysseus' bow sings, before killing the suitors.

In the archaic and classical period, rhapsodes recited Homeric epic without musical accompaniment: the image in the simile did not therefore match how ancient audiences experienced the

Odyssey at the Panathenaea or other festivals of that kind. Still, the Greeks imagined that Homer was a singer—just like the bard in the simile. Three different layers are therefore superimposed: the rhapsode reciting this scene in front of an audience (and we can just imagine how a performer could enact the scene even without an actual lyre in his hands), the mythical author of the poems, and Odysseus as he strings his bow. There could be no better illustration of epic presence. As we read, we are right there, with Odysseus, but also with all the successive audiences who listened to his story.

Chapter 5
The wrath of Achilles

An unusual Greek word, *mēnis*, opens the *Iliad*, and functions almost as its title. Right at the start, we are promised a grand poem about a very specific issue: the wrath of Achilles, which brought countless agonies upon the Achaeans. We are told the cause of this wrath—an apparently petty quarrel between Achilles and Agamemnon, 'leader of men'—and are confronted with its devastating consequences:

> Sing, goddess, the wrath of Achilles, Peleus' son,
> the accursed wrath which brought the Achaeans countless
> agonies and hurled many mighty shades of heroes into Hades,
> causing them to become the prey of dogs and
> all kinds of birds; and the plan of Zeus was fulfilled.
> Sing from the time the two men were first divided in strife—
> Atreus' son, leader of men, and glorious Achilles.
> Which of the gods was it who set them to quarrel and fight?

It was Apollo, we are told, who first caused the quarrel. He too felt 'wrath' at Agamemnon (*mēnis* again), and the reason was this: after a successful raid on a city near Troy, Agamemnon was allocated a captured girl, Chryseis, as his slave. Her father, however, a priest of Apollo, arrived at the Achaean camp as a suppliant, and entreated Agamemnon to release his daughter in return for ransom. Agamemnon refused. Apollo responded with wrath at this show of disrespect. He descended from Olympus 'like nightfall', positioned himself at some distance from the camp, and began shooting his arrows: at first, mules and dogs began to die, but soon the plague spread to the men. Pressure mounted on Agamemnon to release Chryseis, appease the god, and thus put a stop to the epidemic. Achilles spoke out, insisting on what needed doing. Agamemnon agreed to return Chryseis to her father, but demanded to be given Achilles' own slave girl, Briseis, in recompense. This, in turn, enraged Achilles. He considered killing Agamemnon there and then, but on second thoughts (or, as Homer would have it, at the intervention of Athena, goddess of tactics), decided to withdraw from the fighting instead. Achilles' divine mother, the sea nymph Thetis, entreated Zeus to let the Achaeans perish on the battlefield for as long as her son stayed out of the war: Agamemnon would soon realize that he could not afford to insult Achilles.

At the beginning of the *Iliad*, Achilles behaves very much like an insulted deity. The parallels with Apollo, in particular, are clear—not just at the level of language (a rare term for 'wrath' is used for both), but also at the level of structure. When Apollo feels insulted, he sends a plague, decimates the army, and thereby puts pressure on commander-in-chief Agamemnon, who needs to make amends. When Achilles feels insulted, he too ensures that the Achaeans perish, and thereby makes his point to Agamemnon. But from then on, the two cases take different courses. When Apollo obtains what he wanted, he is appeased: Agamemnon releases Chryseis, and the plague comes to an end. By contrast, when Agamemnon finally offers to return Briseis to Achilles, together with countless other gifts, Achilles is still not at all appeased—indeed, he seems 'driven to even greater arrogance'.

The crucial moment of negotiation between Achilles and Agamemnon takes place in book 9. The Achaeans have been suffering heavy losses, and Agamemnon now knows that he needs to get Achilles on side—or else lose the army, his honour, and the war. He sends to Achilles an embassy of carefully chosen envoys: Odysseus, the most persuasive speaker; Ajax, strongest warrior after Achilles; and Phoenix, an old man who looked after Achilles when he was little, and is therefore well-placed to give him advice. They tell Achilles that Agamemnon is not only ready to return Briseis, but is prepared to add many other gifts besides. The women, cities, tripods, animals, and other goods that Agamemnon offers, together with the hand of one of his own daughters in marriage, constitutes a transfer of honour of quite unprecedented proportions. And still, Achilles refuses to return to the battlefield.

The question is why. With Apollo, the situation was clear: Chryseis needed to be returned to her father. With Achilles, it is not at all obvious what, if anything, would put an end to his wrath. Some commentators point out that Agamemnon fails to apologize, and does not make his offers in person—but, then, it may be prudent to avoid a face-to-face confrontation, given how angry Achilles still is. The failure of the embassy cannot be ascribed to Agamemnon alone, or indeed to his envoys. Odysseus, it is true, irritates Achilles, who accuses him of duplicity. The two men suffer from a deep, mythological incompatibility: Achilles needs to choose between glory and a safe return home, as he himself points out to Odysseus; whereas Odysseus famously manages to secure both. Ajax fares better with Achilles, who appreciates his to-the-point talk of duty, and Phoenix inspires genuine affection in him. And yet Achilles still refuses to cooperate—for reasons he articulates with alarming clarity:

> …I do not think
> that anything is of equal worth to my life, not even all the wealth
> they say that Troy, that well-populated city, once possessed
> in time of peace before the sons of the Achaeans came,
> nor all the wealth that the stone threshold of the archer
> Phoebus Apollo guards inside his temple in rocky Pytho.
> Cattle and flocks of sturdy sheep can be got by raiding, and
> tripods and herds of chestnut horses can be made one's own,

but raiding and getting cannot bring back a man's life
when once it has passed beyond the barrier of his teeth.

The prospect of death makes Achilles intractable. Apollo may be
content with amassing gifts 'in rocky Pytho' (a rare Iliadic
reference to his sanctuary at Delphi); but the mortal Achilles must
guard something far more precious to him than any amount of
wealth: his life.

It turns out, then, that Achilles' wrath is not quite like that of a
god, and this was, on reflection, already implied in the first line of
the *Iliad*: 'Sing, goddess, the wrath of Achilles, son of Peleus'. In
the course of the poem, Achilles comes to realize that he is indeed
the son of a mortal man, even if at the beginning he acts very
much like the offspring of his immortal mother. When
Agamemnon insults him, he immediately has an audience with
Thetis, and reminds her that Zeus owes her a favour:

> Mother, I often heard you boasting in the halls of my father,
> when you said that you alone among the immortals
> averted ugly destruction from Zeus of the Dark Clouds,
> at the time when other Olympians, Hera and Poseidon
> and Pallas Athena, were wishing to tie him down.
> But you, goddess, came and released him from his bonds,
> ...
> Sit beside Zeus now, supplicate him, and remind him
> of this, to see if he will agree to help the Trojans by penning
> the Achaeans in by their ships' sterns along the seashore and
> killing them; so that everyone may take delight in their king,
> and that the son of Atreus, wide-ruling Agamemnon, may come to
> know his delusion, in that he did not honour the best of the Achaeans.

The incident mentioned by Achilles features only here, at the
beginning of the *Iliad*, but there is an important background story
that helps to explain Thetis' hold on the supreme god. At some
point in the past, before the Trojan War, Zeus wanted to have sex

with Thetis, but was warned that Thetis' son would become stronger than his father—and so, in order to preserve his own supremacy, he married her off to a mere mortal. That, in Thetis' view, was humiliation enough, and in the *Iliad* she is adamant that her poor son should not now also have to swallow the insults of an Agamemnon. Given that Zeus owes his power to Thetis, he should ensure that Achilles is properly honoured.

The plan on which Zeus and Thetis agree at the beginning of the *Iliad* works out: the Achaeans perish, and Agamemnon comes to realize that he needs to honour Achilles. By then, however, Achilles' own priorities have shifted. He insists that he is not like Apollo, happy to amass offerings at Delphi: he wants to live, and Agamemnon can offer him nothing as precious as life itself. This seems a clear enough answer but, as well as outlining the details of Agamemnon's gifts, the envoys also use other arguments, which cannot be as easily dismissed. Phoenix points out that the gods let go of their anger not just in return for gifts, but also because men need help, and express their need in entreaties and prayers. Ajax reminds Achilles of his duties towards the men on whose side he is supposed to be fighting. These are important arguments, even if Achilles is not ready to accept them yet. He tells Ajax, quite candidly, that he agrees with everything he says, but that he feels too angry when he remembers what happened, and how Agamemnon treated him.

Still, Ajax manages to extract one concession: Achilles admits that he may indeed return to the fighting, when Hector reaches the camp and threatens to set the ships on fire—or rather when he reaches Achilles' own ship, he specifies in a final selfish flourish. For all that, it is clear that our hero does in fact feel some connection with the men who are being massacred on the battlefield. Already in book 11, when he notices the wounded returning to camp, he sends his closest companion, Patroclus, to make enquiries about the fighting. His friend returns with terrible news, and asks Achilles to let him, at least, return to the battlefield. Achilles hesitates, worried about Patroclus' own safety, but eventually agrees to his request, and lends him his own armour as protection. Soon after, Hector kills Patroclus and takes Achilles' armour as spoils. Racked by grief and guilt, Achilles is ready to fight again. His attitude to Agamemnon has not changed (as several details in the narrative make clear), but revenge now matters to him more than life itself.

Just like his anger, Achilles' desire for revenge is exceptional in its intensity and duration. He sacrifices twelve Trojan prisoners on the tomb of Patroclus, and after he has killed Hector continues to defile and mutilate his corpse, denying him burial. Apollo finds his behaviour inhuman and inexcusable:

> ...Achilles has killed pity, and there is no respect in him,
> respect that both greatly harms and also benefits men.
> Someone else will have lost a person even dearer
> to him than this, a brother born of the same mother, or even a son,
> but in the end he gives up his weeping and lamentation,
> because the Fates have placed in men a heart that endures; but
> this Achilles first robs glorious Hector of his life and then ties him
> behind his chariot and drags him round the burial-mound of his
> dear companion. Yet he should know that there is nothing fine
> or good about this; let him beware of our anger, great man
> though he is, because in his fury he is outraging mute earth.

In Apollo's view, Achilles should start to consider his pain in relation to that of other mortals. It may even be that his suffering at the death of Patroclus is not as great as that of a man who loses a brother, or a son. Later in book 24, Achilles comes precisely to that realization—when he sees Priam, and thinks about the imminent bereavement of his own father.

Apollo's remarks suggest that Achilles may not be such a special case, after all. His wrath is devastating, but his confrontation with death is something we all recognize. There are, in fact, many parallels for the story of Achilles—some embedded in the poem

itself, and others originating further afield. In book 9, Phoenix
tries to persuade Achilles to return to the fighting by citing the
example of Meleager, a man who lived 'a long time ago'. This
Meleager initially refused to take part in a war, out of anger, but
was eventually persuaded to defend his wife and home. Quite how
hard Phoenix and, indeed, the poet of the *Iliad* press the details
of Meleager's story in order to turn it into a fitting example for
Achilles is something that scholars have long debated: it can be no
coincidence, for example, that Meleager's wife is called Cleopatra
in the *Iliad*, a name made up of the same elements as Patro-clus
(recalling 'father' and 'glory').

In his grief at the death of his friend, Achilles also resembles the
great Babylonian hero Gilgamesh—another parallel that has
attracted much scholarly debate, since it suggests Near Eastern
influences on Greek narrative traditions. The *Epic of Gilgamesh*
parallels the *Iliad* not just in some striking details, but in its
overall conception. Like Achilles, Gilgamesh is of mixed human
and divine ancestry; like Achilles, he rebels against the human
condition: when his closest friend Enkidu dies, he resolves to go in
search of eternal life. His heroic quest, however, is destined to fail.
In the Old Babylonian version of the story, a wise ale-wife named
Siduri tells him as much towards the end of his journey, and offers
him good advice:

> O Gilgamesh, where are you wandering!
> The eternal life you seek you will not find.
> When the gods created mankind,
> they appointed death for mankind,
> they kept eternal life for themselves.
> So you, Gilgamesh, let your stomach be full,
> day and night keep enjoying yourself,
> every day arrange for pleasures.
> Day and night, dance and play,
> and let your clothes be clean.

Keep your head washed, and bathe in water,
appreciate the little one who holds your hand,
let your wife enjoy herself in your lap.

In the extremity of his pain, Gilgamesh is very far from heeding
those words. Immediately after Enkidu's death, he tears out his
hair, casts off his fine clothes, and roams in the wilderness
wearing an animal skin. And he continues to travel until he finds
Utnapishtim, the only man who survived the flood. It is only
then that he learns a fundamental lesson. The antediluvian
Utnapishtim tells him that he will never find the secret of eternal
life, and then (in the Standard Babylonian version) sends him
home with a fresh set of clothes.

When Patroclus dies, Achilles' physical reaction resembles that of
Gilgamesh. He smears his face and clothes with ash, tears out his
hair, and cries out in anguish. Thetis, who has already started
lamenting Achilles' own death in her submarine realm, hears him,
and comes to his aid. Achilles now wants to fight, she realizes, and
avenge his friend by killing Hector. Even though Thetis warns him
that he will die himself soon after exacting his revenge, Achilles no
longer cares. He has lost his taste for life. He cannot sleep, has no
appetite, and thinks only of Patroclus. As several details in the
narrative make clear, nobody else matters to him.

Achilles' grief is so closely observed that it has attracted the
attention of clinicians. In an important book, psychiatrist
Jonathan Shay diagnoses him with post-traumatic stress
disorder, suggesting point-by-point correspondences between
Achilles' behaviour and the symptoms displayed by many of the
Vietnam veterans he treated: *mēnis*, in Shay's analysis, shares
important features with the berserk rage experienced by his
patients. In both cases, Shay claims, trauma starts with a
betrayal of what is right, according to the social norms governing

the specific context in which the warrior operates; this leads to a shrinkage of the warrior's moral horizon, and a complete loss of control when something terrible happens even within that reduced compass—typically the death of a close comrade. Like Achilles, many modern combatants continue to experience extreme rage and guilt, long after the events that triggered their berserk violence.

There are, of course, limits to broad, transhistorical comparisons of this kind: Achilles is not quite like Gilgamesh, nor are US veterans quite like Achilles. And yet the *Iliad* strives to express an essential quality of human life, and it is therefore not surprising that it resonates, at least in part, with the experiences of people of different times and places. Indeed, the poem insists that Achilles' grief is far from unique. When Priam, king of Troy, hears that his son Hector has been killed, he falls to the ground and covers himself in dung: the gesture expresses how little he now values his own body, and recalls Achilles' own reaction at the death of Patroclus. At the end of the poem, confronted with the problem of human death and bereavement, even Thetis tries to comfort Achilles with entirely human arguments, without appealing to her own divine status or pleading with Zeus. She echoes the advice of the ale-wife Siduri in the *Epic of Gilgamesh*, and indeed the sentiments of countless aspiring grandmothers:

> My child, how long will you eat your heart out with
> grieving and lamentation, giving no thought to food or to
> bed? It is indeed a good thing to lie with a woman,
> since your life will not be long and I shall lose you, and
> already death and your harsh destiny stand beside you.

For all his grief, Achilles does eventually listen to his mother, and sleeps with Briseis. Moreover, when Priam enters his hut as a suppliant, and begs him to release the body of Hector, Achilles is eating. Priam, by contrast, is still feeling the rawest pain at the loss of his son: he has not eaten or slept since the latter's death. In the

10. Marble sarcophagus depicting King Priam as he begs Achilles to return the body of his son, 2nd century CE (*Iliad* 24.477–9). Roman sarcophagus from Tyre, Lebanon, *c.*225–235 CE.

course of their encounter (Figure 10), Achilles persuades Priam to eat, drink, and sleep, telling him the story of Niobe—a mythical mother who lost her twelve children and yet managed (according to Achilles) to have a meal after her bereavement. It seems that Achilles adapts the details of Niobe's tale in order to make his point, but what he says conveys a general truth about life—a truth that Achilles and Priam recognize in each other:

> ...when they had put from themselves the desire for food and drink
> then Priam of Dardanus' line looked in amazement at Achilles,
> seeing how huge and handsome he was, for he seemed like the gods;
> and Achilles too was amazed at Priam of the line of Dardanus,
> seeing his noble appearance and listening to him speak.

After their defilement, hunger, thirst, and exhaustion, these two men share a meal and, in the calm that follows, regard each other. They even 'take pleasure from looking at each other', reaching beyond their personal suffering. The moment does not last: Achilles offers a bed, but Priam sleeps in it only briefly—he wakes up in the middle of the night, suddenly aware that he is surrounded by the enemy, and makes his way home under divine protection.

The *Iliad* does not end with the encounter between Achilles and Priam: the last word belongs to the women of Troy. At the funeral of Hector, which concludes the poem, their ritual laments insist on one crucial theme: their dependence on the man who has just been killed. This is a theme that Achilles, in his great wrath, has difficulty in grasping. From the perspective of the women of Troy, by contrast, it is painfully obvious that people can only flourish if they look after each other.

Chapter 6
A poem about Troy

For all that the word 'wrath' opens the *Iliad*, and announces its theme, the poem is not just concerned with Achilles' destructive anger. Its ancient title (first attested in our sources in the 5th century BCE) promises 'a poem about Troy', or Ilium, another name for the city. As Aristotle points out in his *Poetics*, the *Iliad* focuses on just a small part of the Trojan War, a handful of days: it does not include the fall of the city, or even the death of Achilles. And yet it does manage to become *the* poem about Troy. This cannot have been an easy feat, since we know that many other poems about the Trojan War circulated in antiquity. As already emerged in Chapter 2, the techniques used to compose the *Iliad* were honed over a long period of time, for the purpose of composing and recomposing epic tales in front of live audiences: the point of 'formulaic economy' (that surprising characteristic of Homeric poetry first identified by Parry) was that it aided the process of extemporaneous composition. In short, it was possible to compose many different poems by using the same prefabricated expressions and narrative structures also employed in the *Iliad*. We can therefore deduce the existence of a rich tradition of oral poetry based on the evidence of the *Iliad* alone.

We also know of actual poems dealing with the earlier and later phases of the Trojan War: at some point, these poems were arranged in a 'cycle' around the *Iliad* and the *Odyssey*, and functioned as prequels and sequels to them. We still have fragments of these cyclic poems, as well as useful plot summaries provided by Proclus (5th century CE). We can use them to place the *Iliad* within a wider poetic tradition, but characterizing its relationship with other poems about Troy remains a difficult task.

At the level of detail, it is often impossible to establish whether a specific passage in the *Iliad* alludes to a story already known to its earliest audiences, or whether it represents an initial stimulus for stories that developed in later times. An example may serve to illustrate the point: when Hector meets his mother Hecuba in *Iliad* 6, he expresses deep anger and frustration at the behaviour of his brother Paris, who abducted Helen and caused the Trojan War: he even wishes that he were dead. It would be hard for any mother to hear one son wish death on another, but Hector's words may be particularly wounding for Hecuba if we consider that, according to a story attested for us in later sources, she had actually saved baby Paris from being killed, after a prophecy had predicted that he would cause the fall of Troy. Perhaps the story was already known to the earliest audiences of the *Iliad*; or perhaps it grew around the poem, thereby making it sharper and more allusive in the course of time. Whatever the details and the exact chronology in this particular case, the *Iliad* clearly refers to a wider tradition concerning the fall of Troy—and yet does not rely, for its effect, on audiences recognizing specific allusions.

Rather than rewarding learned readers, who get even the most oblique references, the *Iliad* creates a poetics of inclusion, and that helps to explain its broad appeal. In its relationship to the wider tradition about the Trojan War, it performs a careful balancing act. At one level, it stakes its claim only to a small portion of the story, as Aristotle says: the wrath of Achilles, a few days towards the end of the war. At another, however, it seeks to encompass the whole Trojan saga within its narrow remit.

There are many ways in which the *Iliad* establishes itself as the ultimate 'poem about Troy'. In its structure, it evokes both the beginning and the end of the war. The quarrel over Briseis, in the first book, mirrors the cause of the war itself, since it too started with a fight between two men, Menelaus and Paris, over possession of one woman, Helen. The 'Catalogue of Ships' in book 2 acts as a reminder of the Trojan expedition: it presents all the Achaean contingents, starting in Aulis, the place where they assembled before sailing off to Troy (see map and discussion on pp. 38f.). Book 3 introduces Helen and her two husbands, and explicitly reflects on the origin of the conflict. Book 4 shows how a quarrel over a woman can become a war. In book 5 the fighting escalates, and the gods get involved. Book 6 takes us into the city of Troy, and into the heart of Hector's family. The following books describe the relentless fighting between Achaeans and Trojans, interrupted by the failed embassy to Achilles in book 9, and the seduction of Zeus in book 14.

The fighting continues—killing after killing after killing—right until Patroclus dies and Achilles himself returns to the battlefield. At that point the pace of the narrative changes. Standard arming scenes in the *Iliad* take up a few lines, but now almost half of book 18 is devoted to Achilles' new armour. Similarly, the countless duels described in the poem culminate in the final, extended confrontation between Achilles and Hector, which takes up the whole of book 22. The long narrative of *Iliad* 23 describes Patroclus' funeral, and the athletic games the Achaeans perform in his honour: the poet uses this episode to explore, quizzically and indirectly, several tensions in the Achaean camp—not least between Achilles and Agamemnon (Achilles gives Agamemnon first prize in spear-throwing, without allowing him to compete: 'We already know how much better you are than everyone else'). Finally, in book 24, Priam retrieves Hector's body, and the best Trojan warrior is burned and buried. Hector's death symbolizes the fall of the entire city, as the poet tells us in so many words: 'It was as if the whole of jutting Ilium were now smouldering | with fire all the way from its top to its bottom.'

Apart from encompassing the whole war by alluding to past and future events, another way in which the *Iliad* comes to encompass the whole Trojan War is through its extensive battle narratives, which seem to amount to the entire conflict, even though they describe the killing over only a couple of days. The bulk of the poem is devoted to the action on the battlefield, and this is distressing—not only because the killing is relentless and repetitive, but because it is terrible. Wounds are described in painful detail: a spear enters 'between the genitals and the navel, a place where death is most painful for mortals', another strikes 'at the heart', and quivers for a while to the rhythm of the dying man's pulse; a sword carves out a liver, as 'dark blood fills the man's lap'. Descriptions are graphic, rather than grotesque. Medical evidence confirms that Homeric wounds are accurate: even the weapon that shivers to the heartbeat is documented in modern clinical records. Homeric deaths have their roots in experience, it seems, rather than gruesome fancy.

Each man dies in a particular way. Each has a name, a family, and a specific life that has been cut short. There is no 'unknown soldier' in Homer: every casualty is named. Usually other details are added too—at the very least the patronymic, the name of the man's father. In some cases we are told that the specific father in question is still alive:

> Retreating, Meriones let fly a bronze-tipped arrow at Harpalion,
> and hit him in the right buttock; the arrow passed
> straight through his bladder and came out under the pubic bone.
> Harpalion collapsed on the spot and breathed out his spirit
> in the arms of his companions, lying stretched out on the earth
> like a worm; and the dark blood flowed out, and soaked the ground.
> The great-hearted Paphlagonians busied themselves about him,

and setting him in a chariot carried him to sacred Ilium,
grieving, and with them went his father, weeping tears.
There was no compensation for the death of his son.

Projects and relationships are interrupted by death. Protesilaus,
the first Achaean warrior to disembark on Trojan soil, is killed
straight away, and leaves a young wife in a 'half-built house'.
Axylus, killed by Diomedes, 'used to live in Arisbe, by the main
road, and entertained everyone, yet not one of his guests could
save him'. Lycaon's mother cannot wash him, lay him on a bier,
and mourn for him, because his corpse is thrown into a river
and 'fish heedlessly lick its wounds'.

The poet may offer only some brief details—but we have the
impression that he could tell us more. Just as with Homeric
allusion more generally, there is no sharp distinction between
tradition and innovation when describing the life and death of
individual warriors. In the case of some men, audiences may
know more than the poet chooses to tell (as with Protesilaus, for
example). In the case of others, it seems that the poet brings them
to life precisely at the moment when they are killed: there is no
need to suppose that Axylus, for example, was known from other
epic tales. The overall effect, in any case, is the same. Whether the
poet resorts to allusion or invention, we are made painfully aware
that every death is the loss of a specific man, about whom there
would be more to know.

Poetry becomes a way of paying homage to the war dead: Alice
Oswald captures this aspect of Homeric epic in her poem
'Memorial'—a recasting of the *Iliad* in the form of a list of
casualties. Sometimes, the poet offers a memorable image:

> Ajax, son of Telamon, stabbed Imbrius with his long spear,
> below the ear; he wrenched the spear out, and Imbrius toppled
> like an ash-tree that is felled by the bronze on a tall
> mountain peak and scatters its tender leaves down to the ground.

The Byzantine scholar Eustathius testifies to a long tradition of commentary on these lines: 'The comparison is moving,' he says, 'the poet speaks as though he sympathized with the tree: so say older writers.' Sympathy for the tree also speaks of sympathy for the fallen man. At other times, the poet offers only a matter-of-fact description, such as 'the sons of Antenor, at the hands of king Agamemnon', and yet the sense of loss is palpable. At the level of narrative structure, every killing fulfils the plan of Zeus. Each Achaean casualty makes Achilles' point to Agamemnon. But, at another level, the battle scenes are so extensive, and the deaths so numerous, that the poem comes to represent the entirety of the Trojan War.

Just like its battle scenes, the moral issues explored in the *Iliad* are both general and specific. Achilles asks whether any amount of recognition can compensate for death. His question has special force, since he alone knows for sure that he can either have glory or a long life. Other men can hope for both, and yet they too face the prospect of death as they enter the battlefield. They too need to ask what reasons they have for risking their lives. For some, the answer is straightforward: they fight to defend their households. For others, the situation is less clear. Glaucus and Sarpedon, for example, join the war as Trojan allies from far away Lycia. In a famous speech, Sarpedon explains why they should face danger, rather than enjoy a comfortable life back home:

> Glaucus, why are we two especially honoured in Lycia
> with the best seats and cuts of meat, and ever-full wine cups,
> and all men look on us as if we were gods; and we
> enjoy a huge estate, cut out beside Xanthus' banks,
> fine land, of orchards and wheat-bearing ploughland?
> That is why we must now take our stand in the first rank
> of the Lycians, and confront the scorching heat of battle,
> so that among the close-armoured Lycians men may say:
> 'Certainly those who rule us in Lycia are not without glory,

these kings of ours, who eat fattened sheep and drink
choice honey-sweet wine. There is also noble valour in them,
it seems, because they fight in the first ranks of the Lycians.'
My dear friend, if we two could escape from this war
and were certain to live for ever, ageless and immortal,
I would not myself fight in the first ranks, nor
would I send you into the battle where men win glory;
but now, since, come what may, death's spectres stand over us
in their thousands, which no mortal can flee from or escape,
let us go forward, and give the glory to another man, or he to us.

Honour and glory depend upon the ability to fight in the first line
of battle. But it only makes sense to fight because death is what
awaits mortals anyway, and in every case. Sarpedon's expression of
what scholars call the 'heroic code', the exchange of valour for
social prestige, is predicated upon mortality—and it applies to all
warriors, even if Achilles' case tests its limits, since he knows for
sure that he cannot both enter the battlefield and survive the war.

Apart from the 'heroic code', there is also another code which
characterizes both the Trojan War and Achilles' specific
predicament. Leaders are supposed to look after their people: they
are even called 'shepherds of the people' in a standard Homeric
formula. Again, Achilles tests the limits of this 'people's code'. The
first lines of the *Iliad* point to a scandal, after all: he inflicts
'countless agonies' upon the Achaeans, the men on whose side he
is supposed to be fighting. In his wrath, Achilles plans the
destruction of his own side; other leaders in the *Iliad*, by contrast,
lose their people out of incompetence, selfishness, or even a sense
of shame. Agamemnon's insults cause a plague, and his unfair
treatment of Achilles leads to terrible losses on the battlefield.
Meanwhile, on the other side, Hector cannot protect his city, and
gets killed instead. Leaders fail in the *Iliad*, and the people die as
a result. Homeric audiences must have enjoyed the great tales of
those who fought at Troy, but also felt great relief that they were

not actually fighting at the command of an Agamemnon, or an Achilles, or even a Hector—for all that the latter, at least, did feel a clear sense of responsibility towards his people.

The ruins of Troy loomed large on the coast of Asia Minor, in the 8th century BCE, and will have inspired many different epic tales about the city and its destruction (see Chapter 3). Among those tales, the *Iliad* becomes *the* 'poem about Troy' for several reasons. It offers an intense exploration of leadership and its failures—and in that sense it was very much a political poem. But it also is an existential poem: it confronts death, killing after killing, victim after victim, bereavement after bereavement, and thus invites a clear-sighted reflection on the value of life.

Chapter 7
The tragedy of Hector

Structurally, the death of Hector becomes a symbol for the fall of Troy, but the *Iliad* does not allow us to view it only from that general perspective. The poem explores how Hector himself comes to realize that he is about to die. Achilles has to choose between glory and a long life, and Patroclus dies suddenly, never realizing what hit him. It is only through the figure of Hector that we are shown in detail what it means to draw ever closer to death. This is no coincidence: just as in a Greek tragedy, where the audience need some critical distance in order to confront their worst fears, so too the *Iliad* makes us experience the nearing of death by focusing on a Trojan character, rather than one of the Achaeans. There are also other ways in which the story of Hector resembles a tragedy. He is an impressive character, and yet has flaws, including his acute sense of shame. He deserves sympathy, yet the gods abandon him. Above all, the poet gives us unprecedented access to his state of mind, and contrasts his hope with what we already know will happen to him.

From the point of view of Homeric audiences, there is never any doubt that Troy will fall, that Hector will die, that Achilles himself will die soon afterwards. The poet's divine inspiration—his ability to know the past, the present, and the future—works together with the audience's knowledge of the poetic tradition to which the

Iliad belongs. Although that tradition is flexible, and its contours malleable, certain basic facts are never in doubt. From the point of view of the characters inside the story, however, the situation is different. They may predict the fall of the city, and fear their own imminent death, but the future is not entirely determined: even Achilles occasionally deludes himself, claiming he may still choose to live to a ripe old age.

The distance between what we know—whether we call it fate or epic tradition—and what the characters hope and fear is expressed with special force at the end of the poem, when Hector and Achilles face each other in single combat. Until the very last moment, Hector hopes against all hope that he might kill Achilles: it is that state of mind that gives him the strength to stop running away, and make a stand against the best of the Achaeans. For Hector, then, the future remains at least marginally open, right until Achilles drives his weapon into his body, 'between collar bone and neck'. It is only then that he sees what will happen with prophetic clarity, and tells his opponent that he too will soon be killed, by Paris and Apollo. Later sources fill in the detail: Achilles will be killed by an arrow shot by Paris, and driven by Apollo into his vulnerable heel (see Figure 11).

Hector's words are precise and final: we immediately recognize them to be true. Achilles, by contrast, dismisses them out of hand: 'You die now: as for my death, I will accept it whenever Zeus | and the other immortal gods decide to deliver it.'

Like Hector's prediction, Achilles' words are also immediately recognizable to us: in this case, they are not prophetic, but fallibly human. We are all prepared to believe that we shall die 'whenever'; what we do not want to know is exactly when or how. Like all mortals, Achilles needs to hold on to his ignorance of the future. And yet, in the *Iliad*, it is above all through Hector that we experience both the futility and the importance of hope.

11. The death of Achilles, depicted on a red-figure vase, Niobid Painter, *c.*460 BCE. Paris shoots an arrow, and Apollo directs it towards Achilles' heal.

Already in book 6, when Hector meets his wife Andromache, we are shown how necessary it is to imagine that things may be different and better in the future. At this point in the narrative, despite Zeus' promise to Thetis, the Trojans are losing badly, and the fall of the city seems imminent. Hector rallies the troops and manages to arrest the Trojans' dismal retreat; he then rushes into the city to ensure that the women contribute to the war effort: they should pray, make an offering, and promise a sacrifice to Athena. Hector's expedition into the city is presented as a test of his resolve. He needs to deliver his message quickly, and return to the battlefield as soon as possible, given how badly the army need him. On entering the city, however, he is immediately detained by a crowd of women asking after their dear ones: the poet tells us in an aside that many are already widows or orphans without

67

knowing it, but Hector refuses to give specific information, and tells them all to pray.

Soon, he meets his own female relatives, and they also try to detain him. His mother Hecuba offers him wine, claiming that it will fortify him, given how tired he is; but Hector declines and moves on, insisting that wine would actually sap his strength. He then rushes to see his brother Paris, and tells him to return to the battlefield (he has been in bed with Helen). While he waits for Paris to get ready, Helen addresses Hector in tones of deep regret: she wishes she had died in infancy; but, she adds, given that she is alive and in Troy, she wishes at least that she had a better husband—someone responsible and brave, rather than the useless Paris, who is not quite right in his head. She then invites Hector to sit with her a while, and rest, given how tirelessly he fights on her behalf. Hector rejects her invitation, suddenly claiming that, really, he ought to go and see his own wife.

After the dangers of wine and seduction, Hector now faces his hardest trial: the despair of Andromache. He does not find her at home, and assumes she must have gone to see some relatives, or to the temple ('respectable reasons for leaving the house' as an ancient commentator put it). The housekeeper disabuses him of the notion: Andromache rushed out to the rampart, mad with anxiety, to scan the battlefield, and reassure herself that Hector is still alive. A nurse ran after her, carrying baby Astyanax. Hector now leaves the house, and runs through the streets of well-built Troy, towards the battlefield. Andromache intercepts him at the Scaean Gates (see Figure 12, one influential depiction of their encounter).

When his wife, son, and nurse stand in front of him, Hector turns his gaze to the baby and 'smiles in silence'. Andromache, for her part, addresses him in a manner that recalls the conventions of a funeral lament: she tells him what will happen to him, to her, and to baby Astyanax—should he go out and fight. From our perspective, she foreshadows the end of the poem, since the *Iliad*

12. Angelika Kauffmann, *Hector Taking Leave of Andromache*. When Kauffmann exhibited the painting in 1769, she was accused of turning the Trojan hero into 'a wistful juvenile who wears his helmet uneasily'. The *Iliad* already dramatizes the risk that women pose to Hector's martial resolve.

closes precisely with the funeral laments for Hector. From her own perspective, however, she enacts one possible future, only in order to propose an alternative:

> Hector, you are my father and my revered mother
> and my brother, and you are my tender husband;
> come, show me pity, and stay here on this tower, and
> do not make your son an orphan and your wife a widow.
> Station the people beside the fig tree, where the city
> is most easily scaled and the wall is open to assault—
> three times their best men have made an attempt there.

Ancient readers expressed outrage at Andromache's suggestion, and it has to be said that she violates the very language of epic. Homeric leaders, as has already emerged, should act as good shepherds, and protect their people, not turn them into human walls for Troy, while they stay safely inside. One ancient critic commented: 'Andromache gives counter-military advice to Hector'. Another critic defended her, claiming that her speech was 'not typical of women, but typical of her ... because she loves

69

Hector'. In his own notes on the *Iliad*, Alexander Pope agreed with that latter comment, and pointed out that Andromache did not talk like a soldier, but like a woman who tries to keep her husband safely close to her by engaging him in a conversation about tactics.

Hector, in any case, refuses to be drawn into the details of Andromache's plan: he simply claims that 'all those things' are on his mind too, and then declares that he must return to the battlefield. His reasons have the weight of tradition behind them: he would feel shame (*aidōs*) before the men and women of Troy, should he remain inside the city; and he does not want to do so, in any case—he has learnt to fight in the first line of battle, and to win great glory (*kleos*) for his father, and himself. The choice is not between life and death, but between a cowardly death or a glorious one:

> For I know full well in my mind and in my heart
> that the day will come when sacred Troy will be destroyed,
> and Priam and the people of Priam of the fine ash spear.

Hector must fight—not in order to save Troy, but precisely because he knows that Troy will fall anyway. Through Hector's words, Andromache's suggestions about tactics are revealed for what they are: futile attempts to build alternative futures. In the face of imminent destruction, what matters to Hector is dying well, and being remembered for it. He even projects Andromache into the future, casting her in the role of his living memorial: one day she will be a slave, and carry water for some other woman; passers-by will point at her tearful figure, and remember that she was once 'the wife of Hector, greatest of the horse-breaking Trojans, when they fought around Ilium'. Her pain will, in short, become his future glory. In expressing this thought, Hector finally breaks down: he admits that he had rather be dead, than witness his wife's future suffering. In her own address, Andromache accused Hector of being on a death mission ('your own courage will kill you'), and Hector now confirms this, since he concludes his speech by saying he had rather be dead than see her dragged into captivity.

After that admission, Hector cannot look his wife in the eye, and again turns his gaze to his baby son. He tries to pick him up, but the baby lets out a mighty scream and withdraws into the bosom of his nurse, 'terrified at the sight of his dear father, | the bronze and the horsehair crest nodding | on top of his helmet, a terrifying thing'. Hector and Andromache laugh out loud. A scholiast comments that 'in times of hardship even the smallest incident can cause laughter'. Now Hector takes off his helmet and puts it on the ground, then picks up his baby, throws him about in his arms, and utters a prayer on his behalf. The gesture is familiar: we have all seen fathers lift up their babies, and make them squeal with a mixture of fear and elation. Hector behaves just like any father. And yet his gesture is also a chilling visual reminder of what will shortly happen to Astyanax: after the fall of Troy, another terrifying soldier (an Achaean soldier this time) will pick up the baby and, rather than throw him lovingly about, will hurl him off the walls of Troy, smashing him into the ground below. The superimposition of Hector's last, loving gesture with the enemy's fatal act produces the same effect as Achilles' last words to Hector. We recognize our own human hopes, and simultaneously remember the specific, brutal end of those who died at Troy.

While we are reminded of Astyanax's imminent death, Hector imagines a bright future for his son. Although he has just declared that Troy will fall, now that he holds his baby son in his arms, he cannot but hope. He prays that one day the boy will be stronger than him, that he will bring home the spoils of the enemy, and that Andromache will finally be happy. There is, in fact, no indication that Andromache enjoys the prospect of more wars. When Hector hands baby Astyanax back to her, she smiles and cries at the same time. When she goes back home, she communicates to her servants the desire to mourn for Hector, although he is still alive (an ancient commentator rightly points out that such behaviour is 'beside the norm', a bad omen). Later, when Hector dies, Andromache repeats her initial assessment: he was killed by his own excessive courage. She would have wanted him to die peacefully, in his own bed, holding her hand, and telling her some last, wise word, by which she could remember him: that was her preferred vision of the future, not more wars. The enemy lies beyond Andromache's world view: all she sees, all she can hope to influence, is Hector's own behaviour. From her perspective, therefore, it is indeed his own determination to fight that turns her into a widow.

To an extent, the narrative confirms Andromache's analysis: in book 22, the poet gives us unprecedented access to Hector's thoughts, as he prepares to confront Achilles on the battlefield. All the other Trojans have taken cover inside the city, fleeing 'like fawns' before Achilles' onslaught. Only Hector remains outside, planted in front of the Scaean Gates, 'like a snake full of venom in front of his lair'. We are told what he thinks, as he stands there and 'massive Achilles draws near'. Too many Trojans have died already, he knows. It would be shameful for him to return to the city. Someone would say of him that he has 'destroyed his people' (and here we hear the strength of the 'people's code'). Better to kill Achilles, or die on the plain—than to face shameful reproaches back at home. But perhaps he could just rest his spear on the wall, and try to bargain with Achilles, offer him Helen and many gifts beside. But no, Achilles would not respect him for that, he would kill him right there, unarmed like a woman. Now is the time to fight, he concludes.

Despite this resolution, when Achilles stops in front of him, brandishes his spear, and shines like the rising sun, Hector turns on his heels and runs. Achilles chases, trusting in his swift feet. They speed past the rampart, the fig tree, the wagon road, the fountains where the women used to do their washing, long ago, when the place was safe, before the war. Achilles and Hector are like two athletes competing for the same prize, 'the life of Hector, tamer of horses'. They are like two men in a dream, one running, the other chasing, forever, in an endless loop. Three times they run around the city, but on the fourth Athena intervenes. She takes on the appearance of Deiphobus, Hector's favourite brother, and stands by him. Hector takes courage, thinking that he is no longer alone, and makes a stand.

Achilles now throws his spear, and misses. Athena surreptitiously returns it to him. Hector throws next, and 'does not miss his goal'—except that his spear bounces off Achilles' shield, and lands far away. Hector now shouts out to his brother to lend him his spear, but Deiphobus all of a sudden is 'not by him'. Hector now realizes that he is alone, that the gods have abandoned him, that death is all that remains. The sense of isolation is especially devastating because he has always been at the heart of a community, caring for others. Unlike Achilles who, for most of the *Iliad*, seems concerned only with himself, Hector feels a great sense of responsibility, and is often motivated by what others think of him. And so even now, faced with death, he seeks human contact. He turns to us, future generations who will hear of his *kleos*, his glory, his epic song, and offers us something by which we may remember him:

> Now indeed terrible death is close, no longer far off,
> and there is no escape. So, after all, this is what Zeus and his son
> Who Shoots From Afar have long wanted, they who before this
> were glad to protect me. Now my destiny has overtaken me.
> Let me at least not die without a struggle and without glory,
> but only after doing something great for future generations to hear.

Chapter 8
The man of many turns

Andra, the first word of the *Odyssey*, announces a poem about 'man', and in some ways this is a story about Man *tout court*. The protagonist's quest for knowledge, his travels, his suffering, and his determination to return to his wife and child are all themes of universal significance: the *Odyssey*, like the *Iliad*, seeks to define what it means to be human. But the *Odyssey* is also the story of one, very specific and puzzling man. It is difficult to know what to make of him, or even pinpoint his identity: as the proem builds up, line after line, we are given several details about its protagonist, but we are never told his name. That we are dealing with an *Odyssey*, a 'poem about Odysseus', is therefore something we have to work out for ourselves as we listen to the poet:

Tell me, Muse, of the man of many turns, who was driven
far and wide, after he had sacked the sacred city of Troy.
Many were the men whose cities he saw, and whose minds he learnt, and
many were the sufferings on the open sea he endured in his heart,
struggling for his own life and the homecoming of his companions.
Even so he could not protect them, though he desired it,
since they perished by reason of their own recklessness,
the fools, because they ate the cattle of Hyperion the Sun-god,
and he took away the day of their homecoming. Tell us this
tale too, starting from somewhere, goddess daughter of Zeus.

The first adjective characterizes our man as *polytropos*, 'of many turns'—a word that suggests turns and travels, but also turns and ruses of the mind. Quest for knowledge and travel in space go together: 'many were the men whose cities he saw, and whose minds he learnt'. And yet there is an uncertainty about the weight given to each aspect. Perhaps this is a poem that tracks Odysseus' learning and development, his journey towards a specific goal. Or perhaps this is simply a poem of survival, in which case the protagonist goes through a series of trials and adventures, 'turns' in that sense, and manages to remain unchanged by them all. Return and survival, in short, are not the same thing: return means reaching an end; survival, by contrast, denies death altogether.

Depending on how we see survival and return play out in the *Odyssey*, experiences change—not just for Odysseus, but also for those who listen to his story. If we read the poem as the tale of a man who rejects the immortality offered by the divine Calypso and instead decides to return home, to his mortal wife on rocky Ithaca, there are lessons to be learnt about what it means to be human, and the many limitations that entails. But if this is a story of survival, in which our hero always manages to remain alive, despite suffering the most unlikely and terrible experiences, then perhaps the point of it is not so much learning, but enjoyment. Needless to say, the *Odyssey* offers both pleasure and insight, a story of both survival and return. Balancing those different elements, however, remains tricky, and Odysseus himself remains a tricky character.

As well as being *polytropos*, 'of many turns', he is also *polymēchanos*, 'of many tricks', *polymētis*, 'of many counsels', and *polytlas*, 'much suffering'. These multifarious adjectives are matched by the similes that describe him: Odysseus is compared to a wider range of animals than any other epic hero. As I discussed in Chapter 2, when he faces Nausicaa on the beach he resembles a ravenous and weather-beaten lion—a problematic look, given that he needs to convince her he is harmless. There are other incongruous appearances. Just before meeting her, and after his second shipwreck, he tries to cling on to a rock:

> As when an octopus is dragged from its hiding-place,
> and pebbles cling in thick clusters to its suckers,
> so the skin was stripped from Odysseus' bold hands and
> stuck to the rock; and a huge wave hid him from view.

Later in the poem, he tells the Phaeacians how he survived Scylla and Charybdis, after Scylla had already eaten some of his sailors, and he was passing by the monsters again, on the scant remains of his wrecked ship:

> All night long I floated, until with the sun's rising
> I came to the rock of Scylla and terrible Charybdis.
> Charybdis was now sucking down the sea's salt water,
> but I swung myself upward towards a tall fig-tree, and
> held firmly to it, clinging like a bat; and I could nowhere
> plant my feet firmly nor climb up it, because its roots were
> a long way below and its branches hung far above my head,
> the enormous, long branches that overshadowed Charybdis.
> Still, I hung on grimly, until she should spew up the mast and keel
> once more. I waited anxiously, and they reappeared, but much later,
> at the hour when a man, after judging numerous disputes between young
> men contending for justice, rises from the assembly to go for his supper.
> That was the time it took for the timbers to reappear from Charybdis.
> I let go with my hands and feet and fell from above with a loud
> splash into the middle of her pool, missing the long timbers;
> but climbed on to them and used my hands to paddle myself along.

So it is that, while other men walk home for their supper after a good day's work, Odysseus hangs on to a jutting fig tree 'like a bat'. No wonder it proves difficult to recognize him.

Even when not compared to an unlikely animal, Odysseus takes on many different appearances. He looks 'disgusting' to Nausicaa when she first sees him; but only a little later, after he has taken a bath—and Athena has thickened his hair and broadened his shoulders—the girl thinks he looks like a god. Penelope too, when she first sees her husband again, believes that he is only a pitiful beggar; whereas later, after he has killed the suitors, she considers the possibility that he may be an avenging god. It is only gradually that she begins to see, or admit to herself, a resemblance between the stranger and her husband of old. As for the blinded Polyphemus, he mistakes Odysseus and his men for his own sheep: after trapping them in his cave, the Cyclops lets out his flock to pasture, but checks with his fingers that no men sneak out. What he does not realize is that his prisoners are hidden under the sheep. He even supposes that his sluggish ram is weighed down by sorrow for his blinded master. Recalling the episode, Odysseus triumphantly concludes: 'It was weighed down by me and my cunning thoughts'. (This line, incidentally, is even more striking in ancient Greek, since the word Odysseus uses for 'cunning' also means 'closely packed', and therefore weighty.)

Arguably, Odysseus' most cunning ruse is to call himself 'Nobody' when he first introduces himself to the dangerous Cyclops, thus making his name match his deceptive and changeable appearance. At a crucial point in the narrative, the blinded Polyphemus tells his fellow Cyclopes that 'Nobody is killing him', and so receives no help. Later, when Odysseus tells him who he actually is, Polyphemus remembers an ancient prophecy, and regrets that he did not recognize Odysseus in the stranger who showed up in his cave. Still, he adds, the man not only said that his name was Nobody, but 'looked like a nobody' too.

The appearances and disappearances of Odysseus are not just a matter of tricks on his part, or cunning similes on the part of the poet. They shape Odysseus' very existence, and the plot of the *Odyssey*. In his opening address to the Muse, the poet asks the goddess to start the tale from 'somewhere', and this is the place she chooses: a cave, in the middle of the sea, home of the nymph

Calypso (a nymph whose name, in Greek, sounds very much like the verb 'I shall hide you'). It is a cave that, as mentioned in Chapter 3, cannot be placed on a map. All the other warriors who fought at Troy are either dead or home—except for Odysseus, suspended somewhere between those two states. Calypso offers him immortality, but that would entail remaining invisible, dead to all mortals who once knew him.

The first four books of the *Odyssey* dramatize what Odysseus' state, as the would-be husband of Calypso, means for his actual family back home in Ithaca, poised as they are between hope and despair. His son Telemachus repeatedly declares that his father must be dead, even while he goes in search of him. Penelope, for her part, refuses to hear Phemius' songs about how the other Achaeans sailed home: they remind her of the one return that has not yet happened, and may never occur.

Again and again, Odysseus seems suspended between life and death: after leaving Calypso's island, he reaches the land of the Phaeacians (books 6–12), and then sails home in one of their magical ships—in a state described by the poet as 'a sweet sleep most similar to death'. During his stay with the Phaeacians, Odysseus tells the stories of his earlier travels (books 9–12), and we discover that, in the course of his various adventures, he sailed all the way to the land of the dead, managing to return alive even from there. It was in the Underworld that the prophet Tiresias revealed to him his future: in order to appease Poseidon, Odysseus would have to set off once more and travel to a land where people would mistake his oar for a winnowing fan. That land, that new destination for Odysseus, lies beyond the reach of epic poetry (see Chapter 4). So Odysseus must disappear from view again, as far as Homeric audiences are concerned.

The prophesied continuation of Odysseus' tricks and travels, which lies beyond the end of the *Odyssey*, suggests that his story has no end; that there are ever new adventures, even if we do not know about them all. It is no coincidence that Odysseus mentions Tiresias' prophecy just moments before inviting Penelope to join him in bed: however momentous their reunion, it does not represent the end of his story. Still, our *Odyssey* does of course reach an end of sorts, even if it seems morally and textually unsatisfactory. In his *Poetics,* Aristotle sums up the poem in just a few bold strokes, and suggests a clear purpose and conclusion to it: 'A man is absent from home for many years, is dogged by Poseidon, and is all alone. Moreover, his affairs at home are in such a state that suitors are consuming his resources, and plotting against his son. Then he himself, after being storm-tossed, arrives, reveals his identity to some, saves himself, and destroys his enemies. That is the essence, the rest is episodes.'

This is not how the *Odyssey* is understood today: there is no emphasis on knowledge or travel in Aristotle's summary. Modern perceptions of the poem are surreptitiously influenced by many adaptations, including Charles Lamb's *Adventures of Ulysses* (1808), which transformed the *Odyssey* into an adventure tale for boys, and focused almost exclusively on Odysseus' travels. Aristotle, by contrast, pays attention to the proportions of the Homeric account: halfway through the poem, Odysseus is already back in Ithaca. The second half of the *Odyssey* (the half nobody reads) describes how he regains control of his household and his kingdom, slaughtering Penelope's suitors and their associates. This does not make for comfortable reading. The maids who slept with the suitors are hanged from a rope in the courtyard, as if from a washing line: 'their feet twitched a little, but not for long'. More generally, the confrontation with the suitors and their associates comes close to turning into a civil war.

In the final lines of the *Odyssey*, the people of Ithaca gather in an assembly: half of them support their returned king, while the other half declare themselves against him because he has killed the suitors, who are also their sons, relatives, and friends.

Odysseus himself anticipates the problem in a conversation with Telemachus:

> We know that in any community if anyone kills but one man,
> even one who has no great number to avenge him afterwards,
> that man goes into exile, abandoning his marriage-kin and land;
> but we have killed the bulwark of the city, those who were
> by far the best of Ithaca's young men. You must consider this.

The poem thus reaches an impasse: Odysseus, by his own admission, should leave immediately. It is Athena who saves the situation, through heavy-handed intervention. At the beginning of the *Odyssey*, the goddess discussed Odysseus' case with Zeus, before engineering his return. Now, at the end of the poem, she consults with her father again, before putting an end to the fighting:

Homer

> 'Our father, son of Cronus, supreme among rulers,
> answer my question: what thoughts lie hidden in you?
> Do you intend to prolong this evil war and terrible strife
> even further, or will you bring friendship to both parties?'
> Then in answer Zeus who gathers the clouds addressed her:
> 'My child, why do you ask about this? Why interrogate me?
> Was it not you yourself who conceived this idea, that
> Odysseus should return and take vengeance on these men?
> Do what you wish—but I will tell you the proper way.
> Now that glorious Odysseus has punished the suitors, let
> both parties make a secure treaty: he shall be king for ever,
> and we for our part will cause them to forget the slaying of
> sons and brothers. Let there be friendship between them
> as before, and let peace and wealth be theirs in abundance.'

The supreme god suggests collective amnesia as the only way to restore peace on Ithaca—a proposal that runs contrary to the *Odyssey* itself, since the poem reports the situation and since, more generally, epic poetry is supposed to commemorate the deeds of gods and men, rather than induce forgetfulness.

Athena allows Eupeithes, leader of the opposition, to be killed, but then suddenly orders all men to separate and stop fighting. Terrified, they all obey, except for Odysseus, whose onslaught is only arrested when Zeus himself throws a thunderbolt. The conflict stops, and Athena sets the terms for a peace treaty:

> Then she made a secure treaty between the two sides, for the future,
> Pallas Athena, daughter of Zeus who wields the aegis,
> taking on the likeness of Mentor in both form and voice.

These lines conclude our *Odyssey*, but do not seem to provide a satisfactory ending. Divine intervention is not necessarily the problem: it is a standard feature of Homeric epic. Usually, however, it brings about events that could also be explained with reference to human impulses and decisions, a phenomenon that modern scholars call 'double motivation' (see p. 47 on Athena's restraining effect on Achilles). Already in antiquity Aristotle pointed out that, when divine intervention brings about an unlikely outcome (i.e. an outcome that cannot be explained in terms of plausible human behaviour), this makes for weak poetry. Here, at the end of the *Odyssey*, we are confronted with weak poetry, in his definition: it seems entirely unlikely that a conflict should suddenly stop, after the men involved have already lined up to face each other, and one ringleader has already been killed.

Modern editors have often tried to delete, reshape, or rearrange the various episodes that conclude the *Odyssey*, arguing that they represent different stages or strands of composition, invoking the flexibility of oral poetry, and lamenting the vagaries of textual transmission. Ancient readers were also dissatisfied with the conclusion of the poem: famous scholars working in the library of Alexandria thought that *Odyssey* 23.296, when Penelope and

Odysseus go to bed together, provides a fitting conclusion to the poem. Yet the *Odyssey* does not end there: the flexibility of oral composition and the uncertainties of textual transmission (both of which are in evidence at the end of the epic) testify to the difficulty of concluding a story about Odysseus. The political implications of his actions, and more specifically his failures as a leader, cannot be ignored—for all that Zeus recommends collective amnesia. Indeed, they are explored at length in the poem.

Already in the opening invocation to the Muse, the poet insists that Odysseus should not be blamed for the death of his companions: they ate the cattle of the Sun, and were punished for their own foolishness. Ancient readers rightly asked themselves why the poet focused on that episode alone: the crew of only one ship died after eating the sacred cattle; most of Odysseus' men lost their lives in circumstances for which they were not responsible (see p. 35). For example, Odysseus insisted that he wanted to discover who lived in the cave of the Cyclops, even though his companions begged him not to go there: in the end some of them were eaten, while he survived.

In short, although Odysseus is very different from the great and flawed leaders of the *Iliad*, he too ends up 'destroying his people', to use the Homeric formula. The problem is clearly illustrated by Egyptius, an old man living in Ithaca, who is mentioned in passing at the beginning of book 2. This Egyptius has four sons: one follows Odysseus to Troy, and is cannibalized by the Cyclops; another consorts with the suitors, and is killed in the general carnage of book 22; the other two remain on their father's estate, keep no company at all, and therefore manage to survive both Odysseus' expedition to Troy and his return home.

Of course, Odysseus' loneliness is a crucial part of his story: he is a survivor precisely because those around him die. He appears and disappears because he has no company, no one who holds him constantly in his or her gaze. He is *polytlas*, 'much suffering', precisely because he is alone, has lost everyone, and can rely only on his own resourcefulness. He needs to be *polymētis*, 'of many counsels', and *polymēchanos*, 'of many tricks'. And yet, as his story develops, the words that characterize him shift in meaning, and begin to blend into one another. When he is trapped in the Cyclops' cave, or hangs on to a jutting fig tree for dear life, he has no choice but to endure. When he returns home, however, he chooses to endure various insults and humiliations in order to exact his revenge on the suitors. So it is that, in the second half of the poem, *polytlas* veers in meaning towards *polymētis* and *polymēchanos*: suffering enables dissimulation and, ultimately, victory over the enemy.

Odysseus himself thinks about the links between his past suffering and his subsequent desire for revenge. When Melanthius, a man who serves the suitors, mistreats him, thinking he is just a powerless beggar, Odysseus feels sorely tempted to kill him there and then. Similarly, the behaviour of the maids who sleep with the suitors excites and angers him almost beyond control—yet he manages to hold back, reminding himself that he bided his time even when he was in the cave of the Cyclops. Delayed gratification is, throughout the poem, Odysseus' game. Eventually, the maids are strung up on a rope, like so many 'snared thrushes or doves'; while Melanthius' nose and ears are cut off, his genitals ripped out and fed to dogs, and his hands and feet severed too.

The brutality of the *Odyssey* is shocking, and comes as a surprise to many who read the poem for the first time. It may also have been a surprise in antiquity. Several vase paintings portray Odysseus as a folk-tale trickster, who manages to disentangle himself from all manner of scrapes and misadventures. One vase, for example, depicts him as he flees the north wind Boreas, riding on two amphorae (an episode that does not feature in the *Odyssey*, see Figure 13).

On the vase, Odysseus seems more interested in survival, and perhaps the thrills of a narrow escape, than in leadership or

13. Boeotian black-figure vessel, depicting Odysseus and the wind Boreas, 4th century BCE.

revenge. The *Odyssey* draws from folk-tale traditions recorded primarily in art, but also offers a more disenchanted, epic exploration of power and its consequences. Just as it draws from several different genres and traditions, so it elicits a vast range of responses. By turns a comic character, a tragic hero, a stoic sage, and a villain, Odysseus could never, and cannot yet, be pinned down.

Chapter 9
Women and monsters

For all that Odysseus is hard to pin down, several characters try to do so, particularly women, goddesses, and monsters. They want to keep Odysseus close to them, and make him their husband (or eat him, as the case may be). In a poem so interested in pleasure and family, survival and return, it is perhaps unsurprising that female characters should be prominent: the loneliness of Odysseus, and his constant wanderings suggest that what he needs, above all, is a home. He has one, of course, in Ithaca—but the poem repeatedly suggests that he may set up home somewhere else. His story reflects, in part, the concerns of the age in which the *Odyssey* was composed: the archaic period was a time of rapid expansion, travel, and new settlements. Women travelled less than men, so the scenario in which colonists from far away set up home with local women was readily understandable. Still, women had ways of keeping tabs on their men, and marking them as their own, even when they travelled far.

When Odysseus, disguised as a beggar, first talks to Penelope one evening by a roaring fire, he tells her that he once met Odysseus in Crete, and Penelope immediately asks what clothes this presumed Odysseus was wearing. After some hesitation, the fake beggar obliges her with a surprisingly detailed answer:

> Lady, it is very hard to tell you, when there has been so much
> time in between, for it is now the twentieth year since he

set off from Crete, leaving my ancestral land behind him.
Still, I will tell you what kind of picture my mind has of him.
Glorious Odysseus was wearing a rich woollen cloak,
purple and of double thickness, and on it there was a golden pin
with double clasps, whose front part was cunningly made:
there was a hound gripping a dappled fawn in its forepaws,
holding it down as it struggled. All who saw it were amazed at
how, though made of gold, the hound was gripping the fawn
and throttling it, while the fawn's feet were thrashing as it strove
to escape. Another thing: I noticed the shining tunic he wore,
how it looked like the skin that sits round a dried onion,
so soft it was, gleaming brightly just like the sun; and there
were indeed many women who looked at it with admiration.

The 'beggar' adds that he does not know whether those were the
clothes Odysseus used to wear at home, or whether they were a
gift of some host, 'for Odysseus was loved by many'. Penelope, for
her part, recognizes them at once: those were the clothes and the
pin she had given her husband all right.

That other women admired Odysseus' tunic testifies to Penelope's
skills as a weaver, but also suggests the possibility that these
women admired the man, as well as his clothes. Certainly, in the
course of the *Odyssey*, Penelope is not the only character who gets
to dress (and undress) Odysseus. Before he leaves the island of
Calypso, the goddess gives him a bath and dresses him with
perfumed clothes; a little later in the story, those very clothes
almost drag him down to the bottom of the sea, when Poseidon
wrecks his raft. It is no wonder, therefore, that when the sea
goddess Ino appears to Odysseus shortly after, offering him her
own veil as protection against death, Odysseus thinks twice before
accepting her offer. Her gesture is, as many commentators have
noted, seductive—not least because removing the veil leaves her
exposed to view, so she needs to slither down into the black waves
of the sea rather quickly. Still, Odysseus remains unconvinced by
her offer, and has a long internal monologue about which clothes

he should wear. He decides that, for the time being, he will keep Calypso's clothes and ride on the remains of his wrecked raft, rather than abandon the timbers in favour of veil-assisted swimming, as Ino suggested. It is only as a last resort, after Poseidon tears apart the remaining logs in a second attack, that Odysseus undresses himself, ties the magical veil to his breast, and dives head first into the sea.

Later he washes up, naked, on the Phaeacian coast. The princess Nausicaa has been doing her laundry nearby, because Athena inspired thoughts of marriage in her, insisting on the need for freshly washed clothes: the girl is thus ideally placed to lend the stranger a cloak and tunic, and explain to him how to get to the city. Nausicaa suggests to Odysseus that he should walk with her at first, but keep his distance for the last part of the walk home, in order to avoid malicious gossip. Once in the palace, he should see her parents, and try to please her mother Arete in particular: 'If she has kindly thoughts toward you in her heart, | there is some hope that you will once again see your dear ones'.

Arete's first question to Odysseus concerns the clothes he is wearing: she recognizes the garments that 'she made herself with her handmaidens', and asks him how exactly he came by them. The question of his relationship to Nausicaa could not be more effectively dramatized. And yet it soon becomes clear that the man does not want to marry the young princess. Nausicaa herself ardently wishes he might like to stay and become her husband, and king Alcinous is equally keen to have him as a son-in-law. But Odysseus insists he must leave, so the Phaeacians offer him a safe passage, and many gifts besides. Arete personally gives him more beautiful clothes, and tells him to look after them well, so that they are not stolen when he arrives home. On hearing this, Odysseus 'immediately shut the lid of the chest, fastening it | with a complicated knot Circe once taught him'. Finally, Arete arranges for him to have a bath, and this is 'welcome to his spirit, | for he had not been so cared for | since leaving the home of lovely-haired Calypso'. Odysseus, in short, appreciates the gifts women can offer.

Pleasures are there to be enjoyed, and there are pleasures of all kinds in the *Odyssey*. There is only one constraint on them, it seems: the need to return home. In order to achieve that goal, Odysseus is prepared to accept the most extreme suffering, and even death itself. Otherwise, he seems to feel few constraints. When he first sets off from Troy, he plunders the land of the Cicones, kills the men, and then takes, as he proudly declares, 'their women and possessions, so that none of my men should go without'. When, by contrast, he arrives at the land of the Lotus-Eaters, he forbids his men to taste of the local delicacies as soon as he realizes that the lotus-flower makes them forget their desire to return home.

A little later, on arriving at the cave of the Cyclops, it is Odysseus who wants to find out, at all costs, who lives there, and whether he will offer handsome gifts, whereas his companions suggest they should just steal a few cheeses and make off. In the end, the gift Polyphemus offers to the stranger called 'Nobody' is the privilege of 'being eaten last', a grotesque perversion of the rules of hospitality—but then Odysseus himself abused those rules: ancient guest-friendship was not a matter of wandering into other people's homes, in order to satisfy one's own curiosity and greed, but rather of establishing lasting networks of trust and support. In Odysseus' handling, guest-friendship looks very much like piracy. After leaving the cave of the Cyclops and visiting the wind-god Aeolus, he arrives at the land of the Laestrygonians, and again he sends some scouts ashore to investigate opportunities. Things take a bad turn: the local queen, 'a woman as huge as a mountain peak, a terrifying sight to behold', calls in her husband, who eats one of Odysseus' men, and launches a massive attack on his entire fleet. All ships are lost, except for Odysseus' own.

Not long after this episode, Odysseus meets Circe, and she turns his men into pigs. She would do the same to him, except that he has been given a special herb by the god Hermes, which works as an antidote to her charms. The confrontation between Odysseus and Circe is direct and to the point: she tries to take possession of him by hitting him with her staff, but he draws his sword, and makes her swear she will not harm him before he agrees to climb into bed with her. A year later, when he decides to leave her, Circe tells Odysseus how to reach the Underworld, and how to deal with the Sirens. It is in fact the encounter with the Sirens which, more than any other, pitches Odysseus' pleasure against his *nostos*, his 'journey home'. Desire for the Sirens' song is such that they capture and destroy all who sail by, Circe warns him. In order to protect his men, he therefore plugs their ears with beeswax. As for himself, he asks to be tied to the mast instead—so he can listen to the monsters without being ensnared. This is how he remembers their song:

> ...the Sirens did not fail to notice our
> swift ship drawing close, and they began their clear-voiced song:
> 'Odysseus of many tales, great glory of the Achaeans, draw near;
> bring your ship into land, and listen to our song!
> No man has ever sailed past this place in his black ship without
> hearing the honey-toned voice that issues from our lips, and
> then, full of delight, going on his way a much wiser man.
> You see, we know everything that both Trojans and Argives
> endured on Troy's wide plain, by the will of the gods; and we
> know too all that happens on the earth that nourishes many.'

Knowledge, as the Sirens well know, is a form of pleasure: they promise an *Iliad* to Odysseus, and claim it will give him insight, as well as delight. He is entirely convinced, wants to stay and hear. He even tries to signal this to his men, using his eyebrows, but they only tighten the ropes that tie him to the mast, and bend to their oars.

All the women and monsters Odysseus encounters represent a danger to him. Some are sweet, some are terrifying, but they all impede his return home. Nausicaa, for example, is dangerous precisely because she seems so suitable: many, after all, would choose a young wife and the fertile land of the Phaeacians over an uncertain reunion with Penelope on 'rocky Ithaca'. Odysseus tells the girl all about her charms and the pleasures of marriage, and thus secures her help:

> Three times blessed are your father and your revered mother,
> and three time blessed your brothers! How their hearts must
> grow warm with pleasure because of you, every time they
> see you, such a lovely slip of a girl, going to join the dance!
> But that man must be blessed in his heart beyond all others
> who wins with wedding gifts and takes you home as his bride.
> …
>
> There is nothing better or more powerful than this,
> when a man and a woman keep their house in sympathy
> of mind—a great grief to their enemies, but a joy to those who
> wish them well; and they themselves have the highest renown.

Odysseus speaks the truth, yet deceives the girl. She thinks of marriage with him; he remembers Penelope.

For all the dangerous girls, women, goddesses, and monsters Odysseus meets on his way home, it is Penelope herself who constitutes the greatest peril for him. The story of Agamemnon's return from Troy is told prominently in the *Odyssey*, at the very beginning of the poem and at regular intervals throughout the epic. Clytemnestra took a new husband while Agamemnon was away, and so the Achaean commander-in-chief was killed as soon as he got home. The question of Penelope's fidelity is very much on Odysseus' mind: when he meets his own mother in the Underworld, he immediately asks her whether Penelope still behaves like his wife, or whether she has married someone else.

For Penelope, acting like Odysseus' wife means, above all, arresting time, keeping everything the same until he gets home.

In order to achieve this, she devises the ruse of the shroud: she tells her suitors that she will not marry again until she has finished weaving a robe suitable for Laertes' funeral. Then she weaves by day, and unpicks her work by night. The trick is inventive—practical and symbolic at once. As long as his shroud is still in the making, Laertes cannot die; and as long as the father is alive, there is hope that his son might return. One problem, here, is that Odysseus' own son Telemachus is growing, meanwhile: the *Odyssey* dramatizes the possibility that he might take over as ruler of the household, in which case there would be no need for Odysseus to come back, or for Penelope to remarry (see especially the moment when Odysseus forbids Telemachus to string the bow, discussed on p. 53). Odysseus, it seems, arrives at the last possible moment, just before becoming an irrelevance in his own home.

Once in Ithaca, Odysseus is slow to reveal himself to Penelope, because he needs to test her fidelity. She is likewise slow to accept him back, because she needs to test his identity. Caution is required, for practical reasons, but there is also pleasure in slowing things down. Odysseus and Penelope test and tease each other by rediscovering who they are and what they share—his clothes, for example, and their marriage bed. As a final test for her husband, Penelope casually tells a servant to remove from her chamber the old bed Odysseus made, and he explodes with sudden fury: the bed cannot be moved, he interjects, unless some other man has been tampering with it; he built it himself, and one of its posts is made out of the stump of an olive tree, still rooted to the ground. After that outburst, Penelope finally recognizes her husband. She took her time over it—and thus increased our pleasure.

As for Penelope's own pleasure, the *Odyssey* is coy. There is only one passage, in the poem, which suggests that having many suitors may be enjoyable. When Penelope and Odysseus (still disguised as a beggar) first talk to each other by the fire, she tells the stranger a dream she had, and asks what he thinks about it. In that dream, Penelope was looking at a flock of geese feeding in her yard, and taking great pleasure in them, when an eagle suddenly swooped down and killed them all. In the dream, the carnage left Penelope in tears. But Odysseus is quick to interpret the omen: Penelope should rejoice, he tells her—her husband is about to return.

Chapter 10
An infernal journey

How dull it is to pause, to make an end...

Alfred Tennyson, 'Ulysses'

Of all his many adventures, Odysseus' journey to the Underworld is his most extreme. He manages to reach the place most distant from home, and from life itself, yet return even from there. His *nekyia* in book 11, his 'dialogue with the dead', is arguably his greatest feat, and one that has been replayed again and again in literary history. Still, Odysseus is not the only ancient hero to have visited the Underworld: Heracles, Theseus, and Orpheus also made their descents, and the Babylonian epic hero Gilgamesh learnt about that realm from the descent of his friend Enkidu. Conceiving of death as a journey to a darker realm is, in fact, a common trope in many different mythologies, and the possibility of returning to tell the tale, even from that 'place of no return' (as the Babylonians called it), has been explored in many different traditions.

Each visit to the dead offers its own specific insights and atmospheres. In the *Epic of Gilgamesh*, Enkidu first visits the Underworld in a dream, and learns that our common fate of death erases secular differences of wealth and power: even those who could once share their banquets of meat with the gods now 'eat dust', while their discarded crowns are piled up in a corner of the Underworld. What matters to the dead, Enkidu discovers later on in the poem, is a proper burial and having had many sons in life. Gilgamesh himself crosses the waters of death in order to discover the secret of eternal life from the one man, Utnapishtim, who managed to avoid death altogether—but then falls asleep, and is therefore sent back to his mortal existence. Still, through that expedition he learns the crucial story of the flood from his antediluvian host.

There are also lessons to be learnt from other stories of travel to the world beyond. The myth of Orpheus as told by Virgil, for example, offers a clear warning about the urgency of love, and the damage it can do: when Orpheus disobeys the orders of Hades, and turns to look at Eurydice as she follows him out of the Underworld, he consigns her to the murky world of the shades, and loses her. Odysseus' own expedition seems, as ever, more ambiguous: he learns something specific about his own future, from Tiresias, but as for what we learn, the message seems less clear. The emphasis is squarely on storytelling—its pleasures and advantages, as well as any insights it might offer.

Odysseus tells the story of his journey to the dead while enjoying the hospitality of the Phaeacians, just before securing his passage home. Circe, he recounts, insisted that he needed to consult Tiresias before sailing home, so he and his men embarked on their mission, 'weighed down by anxiety and shedding many tears'. They arrived at the murky land of the Cimmerians by the banks of the river Oceanus. There they pulled up their ship and walked upstream, until they reached a specific place indicated by Circe, dug a trench, and sacrificed to the dead. Immediately, the shades began to swarm up from the Underworld, eager to taste the blood of the slaughtered animals, and 'pale fear' gripped Odysseus. Still, he managed to keep the shades at bay, and did not let them drink the blood. At that point, the shade of one of his companions stood before him: Elpenor could still recognize Odysseus and talk to him, because he had not yet been properly buried—indeed, he had fallen off Circe's roof the night before, stone drunk, and broken his neck. Odysseus addressed him with open curiosity, asking him how he had made it there so fast, faster even than his own swift journey by ship.

As ever, our 'man of many turns' does not seem to take death too seriously, and considers it almost an affront that Elpenor could travel to the Underworld faster than him. Elpenor himself, however, plaintively begs to be buried. Odysseus then spots his own mother among the shades, and yet she does not seem to recognize him. Finally, Tiresias appears, and delivers his prophecy. At this point, Odysseus has accomplished his mission and could therefore leave—but he is curious, wants to interrogate the dead. He lets his mother drink the blood of the sacrificial victims, and she suddenly recognizes him, asking how on earth he made it there while still alive. She then reassures him that Penelope is still faithful, and urges him to tell his wife some good stories when he gets home: 'Go now, make for the light as quickly as you can, but remember | all this, so that some day you will be able to tell it to your wife.'

Odysseus, however, is in no hurry. He sees many famous women, and wants to hear their stories, so he lets them drink of the blood and interrogates them one by one: Tyro who, raped by Poseidon, had to keep her secret while she was alive, but can now talk freely; Antiope, whose sons built the city of Thebes; Alcmene, mother of Heracles; Leda, mother of Helen; Epicaste, mother of Oedipus, who slept with her own son; Iphimede, whose sons (impious giants who tried to reach heaven) were just lovely youths as far as she was concerned; and many other women besides.

On hearing Odysseus' account, queen Arete is enthralled, and asks the Phaeacians not to let Odysseus go away in a hurry, promising more gifts in return. Alcinous likewise urges him to tell more about the dead, and promises Odysseus that he will send him home in the morning, brimming with gifts. Odysseus eagerly accepts the offer, pointing out that arriving home 'with his hands full of riches' would be useful in order to re-establish his rule and authority. After that practical aside, he resumes his tale—a tale which, in Alcinous' view, he puts together 'just like a singer'.

As well as famous women he also saw many dead heroes, he points out, including Agamemnon: the leader of the Trojan expedition asked after his son Orestes, and told Odysseus never to trust women, since his own wife married another and then plotted against his life. Achilles asked after his son Neoptolemus, and urged Odysseus not to 'praise death'; fame was nothing, he insisted, compared to the joys of living—'even as a land-labourer, someone bonded to another man'. And then there was Ajax, who refused to talk to Odysseus, since he had lost a competition against him for the right to own Achilles' weapons. Odysseus urged Ajax to let go of that old resentment (a feeling so strong that it had actually driven Ajax to suicide). He wanted to talk to his old rival—but Ajax refused, and Odysseus soon got distracted. There were, after all, many other famous characters to see: Tantalus, never able to drink water, though it lapped his feet; Sisyphus, forever pushing his stone uphill; Heracles, Theseus, and many others besides. Odysseus would have lingered, and found out more about the dead, but he was afraid that Persephone, queen of the Underworld, might send up the head of the Gorgon (which turned people into stone), so he decided it was time to leave.

Odysseus' *nekyia* shares some features with other ancient journeys to the Underworld: like Gilgamesh, he discovers that people care about burial, and about their sons—even after death. The episode also gives Odysseus a unique vantage point from which to view his own story, not least in relation to that of Achilles. But there is otherwise a curious lack of weight to the episode. Odysseus' mission is complete as soon as he talks to Tiresias, and then he just decides to stay on, first to talk to his mother, and then for the pleasure of conversation with the dead. There is no sense that Odysseus is after something specific, like Gilgamesh's quest for eternal life. In some ways, Tiresias' own prophecy undermines the importance of Odysseus' visit: he will set off on more journeys of discovery, and so communing with the dead is not presented as his ultimate destination. In some ways, his visit recalls his many acts of piracy: what you can get from the Underworld are stories, so he grabs a few, like so many cheeses from the cave of the Cyclops, and makes off before the Gorgon gets him.

Virgil reworked Odysseus' *nekyia* in the sixth book of the *Aeneid*, and in a manner that expressed how profoundly unsatisfactory he found the Homeric account. Aeneas' journey proceeds in reverse order: he walks right past the famous damned—Sisyphus, Tantalus, and characters of their ilk—on his way to more important encounters and revelations. After a well-structured journey he meets his father, rather than his mother, and Anchises reveals a future that does not concern just his own wife and family, but the destiny of the whole Roman people—how they will found a new empire, 'impose a habit of peace, spare the meek, and cut down the mighty'. And Aeneas is in a hurry throughout his stay in the Underworld: there is no sense that he may linger and listen, find out this or that. His visit reveals a higher design, a purpose, a destiny to fulfil.

Dante's *Divine Comedy* is directly inspired by Aeneas' descent into the Underworld, and likewise offers a structured journey. It is, in fact, a supreme Christian effort of organization, where everything finds its proper place—not in our own secular world, but in Hell, Purgatory, or Heaven. Unsurprisingly, Odysseus ends up in Hell, and more precisely in the eighth circle, together with all those who gave fraudulent advice. Sinners in that category are consumed by fire, and find it hard to talk. Still, somehow Dante's Odysseus (or rather *Ulisse*) manages to tell his story, and answer a question that consumed the medieval imagination: how he finally died. Dante tells us that he made his way home, but then could not stay there: burning with desire to become 'expert of the world', he abandoned home and family, and sailed west. At the Pillars of Heracles he delivered a short and rousing speech to his crew: men were not 'meant to live like brutes, but to pursue excellence and knowledge'. And so he sailed west past the strait of Gibraltar into the unknown, and after some five months saw a 'dark and distant mountain', at which point his ship revolved three times on itself, and sank into the ocean.

Dante had no access to the *Odyssey* in Greek, and seems to have ignored the Latin summaries of the poem that circulated in his time. His account was based on ancient Roman authors: from Virgil he knew that Ulysses was an 'inventor of crimes', including the ruse of the Trojan Horse; from Cicero, Horace, Seneca, and others he learnt of his passion for knowledge. The short and ardent speech Ulysses delivers in the *Inferno* expresses his determination to learn, but also demonstrates his ability to give bad counsel, since he incites his crew to travel beyond human limitations set by God. We are given to understand that the dark and distant mountain they see before shipwreck is Paradise on Earth, later to become the site of Purgatory.

The story of Ulysses' death seems to have been Dante's own invention, since the earliest commentators of the *Comedy* remark on its novelty. It must have been inspired by medieval legends about Alexander the Great, but also by real-life explorations (the Vivaldi brothers attempted to reach India by sailing west into the Atlantic in 1291, shortly before Dante wrote his *Comedy*, and centuries before Columbus). Last but not least, Dante must have drawn from his own experience—since he too abandoned family and home during his exile, and later pursued his quest for knowledge rather than settle for a humble apology and return home. Dante's first biographers perceived the similarities between the medieval poet and his Ulysses—in the grandeur of their pursuits, and also in their arrogant descent to Hell.

Even after knowledge of Homeric epic spread to the west (see the Introduction to this volume), Dante's infernal journey continued to colour Odysseus' *nekyia*. Tennyson's 'Ulysses', for example, owes at least as much to his medieval as to his ancient self when he determines 'to strive, to seek, to find, and not to yield'. The influence of Dante can be felt also in the many infernal journeys of 20th-century literature, including James Joyce's *Ulysses* and Primo Levi's account of his descent to, and return from, Auschwitz. Levi's *If This is a Man* includes a 'Canto di Ulisse', in which he describes the urgent need to remember Dante's lines in the *Inferno*, while pulling a cart through the extermination camp. That urge is explicitly set against the foremost preoccupation at Auschwitz, the quest for food: 'you were not made to live like brutes, but to follow excellence and knowledge'. More than insight, even, Levi craved the rhythms of poetry as he carted his load. Levi's Dantesque Ulysses shades into Homer's Odysseus in his memoirs, particularly as he insists that cunning was needed in order to make it out of Auschwitz. *The Truce*, Levi's account of his return home, is Odyssean in both tone and specific detail: there is, for example, a Greek Jew from Salonica, a master trickster who treats even the resourceful Levi as a mere apprentice. There is the uncontrollable need to tell what happened, an urge stronger even than the all-consuming need for food. And finally there is the question whether the survivor is a man—a question that tormented Levi with increasing violence as he lived on, and as he put an end to his own life in 1987.

Many traumatic experiences of the 20th-century echo Odysseus' journey to the dead (see Figure 14). For example, the poets Derek Walcott and Aimé Césaire cast their postcolonial returns to their native Caribbean islands simultaneously as a *nostos*, a return home, and a journey to the land of the dead. Some of their experiences are specific, as when local children ask for money 'because your clothes, | your posture | seem a tourist's', but their insights also expose the lies that Odysseus told all of us. There is no possible return, after all: travel is in one direction only—towards death. And yet. For all the difficulties, for all the unlikely tricks and manoeuvres, there is in the *Odyssey*, in its

14. **Romare Bearden's *Roots Odyssey* (1976) depicts the Middle Passage, the traumatic journey of black slaves from Africa to the Americas, as a journey of the living dead.**

protagonist and his many reincarnations, not just a will to live, but a determination to take pleasure in the tale. And so it is that the *nekyia*, the ancient conversation with the dead, suggests that literature itself may be an inadequate, morally ambiguous, fallibly human, and specifically Odyssean attempt to cheat death.

References

Translations from the *Iliad* and the *Odyssey* are loosely based on Anthony Verity's *Iliad* for Oxford World's Classics (2011), and on his version of the *Odyssey* for the same series (2016). Other translations, unless otherwise stated, are my own.

Introduction

Petrarch claims to have hugged a manuscript of the *Iliad* in *Epistolae Familiares*, 18.2.10. The relevant passages of the letters in which he and Boccaccio discuss Leontius Pilate are collected in A. Pertusi, *Leonzio Pilato fra Petrarca e Boccaccio* (Venice, 1964), 40f. P. H. Young, *The Printed Homer: A 3000 Year Publishing and Translation History of the Iliad and the Odyssey* (Jefferson, NC, 2003) includes a catalogue of Homeric translations up to the year 2000.

Chapter 1: Looking for Homer

Ancient speculations about the meaning of the name 'Homer', and his possible place of birth, are found primarily in the ancient *Lives of Homer*, translated for the Loeb Classical Library by M. L. West (Cambridge, MA, 2003). Aeschylus' statement about taking 'slices from the banquet of Homer' is quoted in Athenaeus 8.347e. Herodotus discusses the authenticity of the *Cypria* in *Histories* 2.117. Aristotle talks about Homer's 'technique or natural genius' in his *Poetics* 1451a24. Pliny mentions the desire to picture Homer's face in *Natural*

History 35.9. Gianbattista Vico complains about Homeric epic being 'vile, rude, cruel', etc. in *New Science* 3.1. Goethe's couplet on Wolf's Homer is published in *Gedenkausgabe der Werke, Briefe und Gespräche*, ed. E. Beutler, vol. 2 (Zurich, 1953), 478. Nietzsche's inaugural lecture is published in *Kritische Gesamtausgabe*, ed. G. Colli and M. Montinari, vol. 2.1 (Berlin, 1982), 247–79.

Chapter 2: Textual clues

Milman Parry claims that Homeric audiences were indifferent to Homeric epithets and that they are best left untranslated in *The Making of Homeric Epic*, ed. A. Parry (Oxford, 1971), 171f. W. Arend, *Die typischen Scenen bei Homer* (Berlin, 1933) coined the term 'type scenes'. Achilles and Apollo clash at the beginning of *Il.* 22; the lines quoted are 8–10, 14–15, and 20. Odysseus emerges from the bushes, covers himself with a leafy branch, and confronts Nausicaa in *Odyssey* 6.127–44. For the ancient notion that Homer knew all the Greek dialects, see M. Hillgruber, *Die pseudoplutarchische Schrift De Homero*, vol. 1 (Stuttgart and Leipzig, 1994), 102–3. The river Caÿster, near Ephesus, is mentioned at *Il.* 2.461.

Chapter 3: Material clues

Ulrich von Wilamowitz-Moellendorff berates Schliemann in 'Über die ionische Wanderung', *Sitzungsberichte der Königlich Preußischen Akademie der Wissenschaften* (Berlin, 1906), 59. Boulders 'that no two men could lift, such as they are nowadays': *Il.* 5.302–4, 12.445–9, and 20.285–7. Homeric similes: *Il.* 11.558–65 (Ajax like a donkey); *Il.* 4.130–3 (Athena like a mother diverting a fly); *Od.* 19.233 (a tunic like the skin of an onion); *Il.* 5.487, 16.406–8, and 24.80–2, *Od.* 10.124 and 22.384–7 (fishing); *Il.* 23.712f. (interlocking beams); *Od.* 6.232–5 (silver overlaid with gold); *Il.* 4.141–5 (an ivory mouthpiece stained with purple). Odysseus' men eat fish to avoid starvation: *Od.* 12.329–32; a 'race of demi-god men': *Il.* 12.23; the cult of Sarpedon in Lycia: *Il.* 16.666–83. Odysseus is blown off course while rounding Cape Malea *Od.* 9.80f.; the magical ships of the Phaeacians: *Od.* 8.556–63; description of Ithaca: *Od.* 9.21–8. For a useful guide to ancient and modern attempts to reconstruct Odysseus' journey, see Jonathan Burgess' collection and discussion of sources at <http://homes.chass. utoronto.ca/~jburgess/rop/od.voyage.html>. R. Bittlestone tries to line up the Homeric description of Ithaca with the geography of the western Greek island by invoking massive earthquakes in *Odysseus Unbound: The Search for Homer's Ithaca* (Cambridge, 2005); for a critical view, see B. Graziosi, 'Where is Ithaca?', *Journal of Hellenic Studies* 128 (2008): 178–80. Demodocus' songs: *Od.* 8.73–108, 256–370, and 474–541; Phemius' performance: *Od.* 1.325–59; a fleeting reference to writing, or something close to it: *Il.* 6.160–70.

Chapter 4: The poet in the poems

The poet invokes the Muses before the 'Catalogue of Ships': *Il.* 2.484–93. Ancient concerns about the proem of the *Odyssey*: scholia g1 to *Od.* 1.8, in F. Pontani, ed., *Scholia graeca in Odysseam* (Rome, 2007–). Demodocus sings about what happened in Troy 'as if he had been there himself', and Odysseus rewards him with a joint of pork: *Od.* 8.471–98. The Muse gives Demodocus sweet song and blindness: *Od.* 8.63f. The singer Phemius begs Odysseus to spare his life: *Od.* 22.344–53. 'Longinus' compares the *Iliad* to the sun at noon, and the *Odyssey* to a sunset: *On the Sublime* 9.12–14. The curved coastline, with its beached Achaean ships, is arranged before the poet 'like a theatre': scholia A (Aristonicus) to *Il.* 14.35a in H. Erbse, *Scholia graeca in Homeri Iliadem* (Berlin: 1969–88). J. Strauss Clay, *Homer's Trojan Theater: Space, Vision, and Memory in the Iliad* (Cambridge, 2011) establishes the position of the poet in relation to the battlefield; a computer simulation based on her work is available here: <http://www.homerstrojantheater.org>. A spear mashes up a brain: *Il.* 12.182–6; two horses stumble, and a whole army flees: *Il.* 6.37–41. The map of the 'Catalogue of Ships' and 'Catalogue of the Trojans' is based on G. Danek, 'Der Schiffskatalog der Ilias. Form und Funktion', in H. Heftner and K. Tomaschitz, eds, *Ad Fontes! Festschrift für Gerhard Dobesch* (Vienna, 2004), 59–72; the arrows refer to the following lines in *Il.* 2: A=494–580; B=581–614; C=615–44; D=645–80; E=681–759; F=816–43; G=844–57; H=858–63; I=864–6; J=867–77. The 'Shield of Achilles': *Il.* 18.478–608; Achilles recognizes the shield as the work of a divine craftsman: *Il.* 19.21f.; his men flee at its sight: *Il.* 19.14f. The sight of Achilles' weapons blinds Homer: *Life of Homer* 7.5 in M. L. West, ed., *Homeric Hymns, Homeric Apocrypha, Lives of Homer* (Cambridge, MA, 2003). Zeus complains about mortals who blame the gods: *Od.* 1.28–43. Poseidon spots Odysseus on his raft from the top of the Solymian mountains, on his way from Aethiopia to Olympus: *Od.* 5.282–4. Tiresias predicts Odysseus' future: *Od.* 11.100–37. Odysseus makes his way to Eumaeus' pigsty: *Od.* 14.1–4. The dog Argos recognizes his old master, wags his tail, and dies: *Od.* 17.291–327. Odysseus removes weapons from the hall: *Od.* 19.1–34; the contest of the bow takes up the whole of book 21. According to Plato, *Ion* 535b, Homeric audiences found the scene when Odysseus leaps on the threshold and starts shooting arrows at the suitors particularly thrilling. The poet compares Odysseus to a singer at *Od.* 21.405–11.

Chapter 5: The wrath of Achilles

The wrath of Achilles (*Il.* 1.1) is matched by the wrath of Apollo (*Il.* 1.75). The god Apollo descends from Olympus 'like nightfall': *Il.* 1.47. Athena restrains Achilles: *Il.* 1.194–222; Achilles is 'driven to even greater arrogance': *Il.* 9.700. Achilles tells Odysseus that it is necessary to choose between glory and a safe return home, though of course Odysseus will achieve both: *Il.* 9.413. Achilles explains the reasons why he refuses to return to the battlefield: *Il.* 9.401–9. Zeus owes Thetis a favour: *Il.* 1.396–401 and 407–12, with L. Slatkin, *The Power of Thetis: Allusion and Interpretation in the Iliad* (Berkeley, 1991). Achilles agrees with Ajax that he should return to the battlefield, but is too angry with Agamemnon to do so: *Il.* 9.644–8. He will resume fighting only when Hector sets the Achaean ships on fire: *Il.* 9.649–55. Apollo finds Achilles' behaviour inhuman: *Il.* 24.44–54. The story of Meleager is told in *Il.* 9.527–99. For Siduri's advice to Gilgamesh, and the *Epic of Gilgamesh* more generally, see A. R. George's critical edition (Oxford, 2003), 278f. Achilles' physical reaction to the death of Patroclus is described at *Il.* 24.1–110. Thetis tells Achilles that he should eat, sleep, and have sex: *Il.* 24.128–32. Achilles and Priam regard each other: *Il.* 24.628–33.

Chapter 6: A poem about Troy

Hector talks to his mother at *Il.* 6.242–85; Euripides' lost tragedy *Alexander* tells the story of how Hecuba rescued Paris from being killed in infancy; see C. Collard and M. J. Cropp, *Euripides: Fragments*, vol. VII (Cambridge, MA, 2008). Achilles grants Agamemnon first prize in spear-throwing: *Il.* 23.889–97. Hector's death symbolizes the fall of the entire city: *Il.* 22.410f. Homeric wounds: *Il.* 13.568f. (between genitals and navel); 13.442–4 (spear quivers to the heartbeat of the wounded); 20.469–71 (a liver slides out of the abdomen). Clinical observations that corroborate Homeric descriptions of wounds are collected in K. B. Saunders, 'The wounds in *Iliad* 13–16', *Classical Quarterly* 49 (1999): 345–63. A father survives his son: *Il.* 13.650–9; a young widow is left in a 'half-built house': *Il.* 2.701; a hospitable man is killed: *Il.* 6.13–16; a mother cannot wash her son's corpse: *Il.* 21.122–4; a warrior falls like a felled tree: *Il.* 13.177–80; Eustathius' comments: M. van der Valk, ed., *Eustathii archiepiscopi Thessalonicensis commentarii ad Homeri Iliadem pertinentes* (Leiden, 1971–87), 926.54. The sons of Antenor are killed by Agamemnon: *Il.* 11.262; Sarpedon sets out the 'heroic code': *Il.* 12.310–28.

Chapter 7: The tragedy of Hector

Achilles claims that he can still have a long life at *Il.* 9.414–16. Hector must die 'now', whereas Achilles will die 'whenever': *Il.* 22.365–6. Hector meets the women of Troy (*Il.* 6.237–41), his mother (6.251–85), Helen (6.343–68), the housekeeper (6.369–89), and finally his wife Andromache and baby son Astyanax (6.392–502). 'Respectable reasons for leaving the house': scholia bT to *Il.* 6.378; 'Andromache gives counter-military advice to Hector': scholia A to *Il.* 6.433–9; 'not typical of women, but typical of her': scholia bT to *Il.* 6.433; 'in times of hardship even the smallest incident can cause laughter': scholia bT on *Il.* 6.471; 'beside the norm': scholia bT to *Il.* 6.499, all in H. Erbse, *Scholia graeca in Homeri Iliadem* (Berlin, 1969–88). Alexander Pope insists that Andromache speaks like a woman, rather than a soldier: M. Mack, ed., *The Poems of Alexander Pope*, vol. 7: 'Translations of Homer' (New Haven, 1967), 354. Hector imagines Andromache as his living memorial: *Il.* 6.460f. Andromache claims that Hector was killed by his own excessive courage: *Il.* 6.407, 6.431f., and 22.454–9. She would have wanted him to die in his own bed: *Il.* 24.743–5. Kaufmann's Hector is dismissed as a 'wistful juvenile': W. Boime, *Art in the Age of Revolution* 1750–1800 (Chicago, 1987), 112f. Achilles draws near, and Hector watches him like a poisonous snake: *Il.* 22.92–5. Hector worries that he will be accused of destroying his people: *Il.* 22.107. Achilles and Hector run like two athletes competing over the life of Hector: *Il.* 22.161; they run as if in a dream: *Il.* 22.199–201. Hector 'does not miss his goal' but needs another spear: *Il.* 22.290–5. Hector makes a final resolution to face Achilles bravely, for our sake: *Il.* 22.300–5.

Chapter 8: The man of many turns

Odysseus looks like a weather-beaten lion (*Od.* 6.130–6), like an octopus (*Od.* 5.432–5), like a bat (*Od.* 12.429–44). He looks 'disgusting' to Nausicaa, but a little later 'like a god': *Od.* 6.137 and 243. He looks 'pitiful' to Penelope, and then she imagines he might be 'an avenging god': *Od.* 19.253 and 23.63. Penelope cautiously admits to herself a resemblance with her old husband: *Od.* 23.94f. Odysseus hangs under Polyphemus' ram: *Od.* 9.425–61. Odysseus looks like a 'nobody': *Od.* 9.515. He sails home while asleep: *Od.* 13.80. Odysseus tells Penelope Tiresias' prophecy, and they go to bed together: *Od.* 23.251–87. Aristotle summarizes the *Odyssey* and complains about implausible divine interventions: *Poetics* 1455b16–23 and 1454b1–6. Odysseus explains to Telemachus the risk of civil war: *Od.* 23.118–22. Athena consults with Zeus: *Od.* 1.44–95 (see also 5.5–27) and 24.473–86. Melanthius provokes Odysseus, and is eventually maimed: *Od.* 17.212–38 and 22.474–7. The maids provoke Odysseus, and are hung: *Od.* 20.6–24 and 22.457–73.

Chapter 9: Women and monsters

Penelope and Odysseus talk about the clothes she made for him at *Od.* 19.213–60. Odysseus is given clothes by Calypso (*Od.* 5.264, cf. 5.320), Ino (*Od.* 5.333–64), Nausicaa (*Od.* 6.228, cf. 7.235), and Arete (*Od.* 8.438–45). Circe's special knot: *Od.* 8.447f. Nausicaa would like to marry Odysseus (*Od.* 6.244f.), and her father agrees (*Od.* 7.311–15); Odysseus enjoys Arete's warm bath (*Od.* 8.450–2). More on Homeric women and clothes can be found in L. G. Canevaro, *Women of Substance in Homeric Epic: Women, Objects, Agency* (Oxford, 2018). Odysseus enslaves and abducts the Ciconian women (*Od.* 9.41f.); forbids contact with the Lotus-Eaters (*Od.* 9.91–102); rejects the opportunity to steal the Cyclops' cheeses (*Od.* 9.224–9); is offered the doubtful privilege of 'being eaten last' (*Od.* 9.369); describes how his men encounter 'a woman as huge as a mountain peak' (*Od.* 10.112f.); and hears the song of the Sirens (*Od.* 12.182–91). Penelope thinks up the ruse of the shroud (*Od.* 2.93–110), the ruse of the bed (*Od.* 23.177–204), and has a dream about geese (*Od.* 19.535–58).

Chapter 10: An infernal journey

Tennyson's 'Ulysses' (1842) is published in *A Selected Edition*, ed. C. Ricks (London, 1989), 138–45. The dead 'eat dust' in *The Epic of Gilgamesh*, Tablet VII; we discover that they care about proper burial, and about having had many sons in Tablet XII: see the edition by A. R. George (Oxford, 2003), 644f., 732–5. Odysseus and his men shed 'many tears' at the prospect of setting off for a journey to the Underworld: *Od.* 11.5. 'Pale fear' grips Odysseus: *Od.* 11.43. He is curious about how quickly people travel to the Underworld after they die: *Od.* 11.57f. Odysseus' mother tells him to leave the land of the dead, and tell the story of his visit to Penelope: *Od.* 11.223f. Arete and Alcinous admire Odysseus' tale, and he admits that their gifts are useful: *Od.* 11.335–76. Achilles tells Odysseus that he should not 'praise death' and that he envies anyone who still lives, even a field labourer: *Od.* 11.488–91. G. Gazis, *Homer and the Poetics of Hades* (Oxford, 2018) discusses Odysseus' encounters in the Underworld in greater and convincing detail. The Romans will 'impose a habit of peace, spare the meek, and cut down the mighty': Virgil, *Aeneid* 6.851–3. Dante's Ulysses wants to become 'expert of the world' (*Inferno* 26.98), and tells his crew that they were 'not meant to live like brutes, but to pursue excellence and knowledge' (*Inferno* 26.119f.). Virgil calls Ulysses an 'inventor of crimes' (*Aeneid* 2.164). Primo Levi remembers his descent and return from Auschwitz in *If This is a Man* (*Se questo è un uomo*, Turin, 1958) and *The Truce* (*La tregua*, Turin, 1963). 'Because your clothes, | your posture | seem a tourist's': D. Walcott, 'Homecoming: Anse la Raye' (1969), 21–3, published in *Collected Poems: 1948–1984* (New York, 1984), 127–9; see also his celebrated long narrative poem *Omeros* (New York, 1990), and A. Césaire, *Cahier d'un retour au pays natal* (Paris, 1939).

Further reading

General

Reference

M. Finkelberg, ed., *Homer Encyclopaedia*, 3 vols (Chichester and Malden, MA, 2011).

Near-Eastern epic and Homeric epic

J. M. Foley, ed., *A Companion to Ancient Epic* (Malden, MA, 2005).

B. R. Foster, *Before the Muses: An Anthology of Akkadian Literature*, 3rd edition (Bethesda, 2005).

A. R. George, *The Babylonian Gilgamesh Epic: Introduction, Critical Edition and Cuneiform Texts* (Oxford, 2003).

J. Haubold, *Greece and Mesopotamia: Dialogues in Literature* (Cambridge, 2013).

M. L. West, *The East Face of Helicon: West Asiatic Elements in Greek Poetry and Myth* (Oxford, 1997).

The tradition of the Trojan War

N. Austin, *Helen of Troy and Her Shameless Phantom* (Ithaca, NY, 1994).

J. S. Burgess, *The Tradition of the Trojan War in Homer and the Epic Cycle* (Baltimore, 2001).

M. L. West, ed., *Homeric Hymns, Homeric Apocrypha, Lives of Homer* (Cambridge, MA, 2003).

Iliad and *Odyssey*

J. S. Burgess, *Homer* (London, 2014).

A. Ford, *Homer: The Poetry of the Past* (Ithaca, NY, 1992).

R. Fowler, ed., *The Cambridge Companion to Homer* (Cambridge, 2004).

B. Graziosi and J. Haubold, *Homer: the Resonance of Epic* (London, 2005).

J. Griffin, *Homer on Life and Death* (Oxford, 1980).

I. Morris and B. Powell, eds, *A New Companion to Homer* (Leiden, 1997).

R. B. Rutherford, *Homer*, 2nd edition (Cambridge, 2013).

S. Schein, *Homeric Epic and Its Reception* (Oxford, 2016).

A. J. B. Wace and F. H. Stubbings, eds, *A Companion to Homer* (London, 1962).

Editions of the *Iliad*

H. van Thiel, ed., *Homeri Ilias* (1996, Hildesheim).

M. L. West, ed., *Homeri Ilias* (1998–2000, Stuttgart and Leipzig).

Ancient and modern commentaries on the *Iliad*

H. Erbse, ed., *Scholia graeca in Homeri Iliadem* (Berlin, 1969–88).

G. S. Kirk et al., eds, *The Iliad: A Commentary* (Cambridge, 1985–93).

M. van der Valk, ed., *Eustathii archiepiscopi Thessalonicensis commentarii ad Homeri Iliadem pertinentes* (Leiden, 1971–87).

M. M. Willcock, *A Companion to the Iliad, Based on the Translation by Richmond Lattimore* (Chicago, 1976).

M. M. Willcock, ed., *The Iliad of Homer* (London, 1978–84).

Secondary literature on the *Iliad* (see also Chapters 5–7)

D. Cairns, ed., *Oxford Readings in Homer's Iliad* (Oxford, 2001).

M. W. Edwards, *Homer: Poet of the Iliad* (Baltimore, 1987).

I. de Jong, *Narrators and Focalizers: The Presentation of the Story in the Iliad*, 2nd edition (Bristol, 2004).

M. Lynn-George, *Epos: Word, Narrative and the Iliad* (Basingstoke, 1988).

R. P. Martin, *The Language of Heroes: Speech and Performance in the Iliad* (Ithaca, NY, 1989).

G. Nagy, *The Best of the Achaeans: Concepts of the Hero in Archaic Greek Poetry*, 2nd revised edition (Baltimore, 1999).

S. Schein, *The Mortal Hero: An Introduction to Homer's Iliad* (Berkeley, 1984).

O. Taplin, *Homeric Soundings: The Shaping of the Iliad* (Oxford, 1992).

S. Weil, *The Iliad or The Poem of Force*, ed. J. P. Holoka (New York, 2003).

Editions of the *Odyssey*

H. van Thiel, ed., *Homeri Odyssea* (Hildesheim, 1991).

M. L. West, ed., *Homerus. Odyssea* (2017, Berlin and Boston).

Ancient and modern commentaries on the *Odyssey*

W. Dindorf, ed., *Scholia graeca in Homeri Odysseam* (Oxford, 1855).

I. de Jong, *A Narratological Commentary on the Odyssey* (Cambridge, 2001).

A. Heubeck, S. West, and J. B. Hainsworth, *A Commentary on Homer's Odyssey* (Oxford, 1988–92).

F. Pontani, ed., *Scholia graeca in Odysseam* (Rome, 2007–).

G. Stallbaum, ed., *Eustathii archiepiscopi Thessalonicensis commentarii ad Homeri Odysseam ad finem exempli romani editi* (Leipzig, 1825–6).

Secondary literature on the *Odyssey* (see also Chapters 8–10)

N. Austin, *Archery at the Dark of the Moon: Poetic Problems in Homer's Odyssey* (Berkeley, 1975).

L. E. Doherty, ed., *Oxford Readings in Homer's Odyssey* (Oxford, 2009).

C. Dougherty, *The Raft of Odysseus: The Ethnographic Imagination of Homer's Odyssey* (Oxford, 2001).

P. Pucci, *Odysseus Polutropos: Intertextual Readings in the Odyssey and the Iliad*, 2nd edition (Ithaca, NY, 1995).

S. Reece, *The Stranger's Welcome*: *Oral Theory and the Aesthetics of the Homeric Hospitality Scene* (Ann Arbor, 1993).

R. B. Rutherford, 'At home and abroad: aspects of the structure of the *Odyssey*', *Proceedings of the Cambridge Philological Society* 31 (1985): 133–50.

S. Saïd, *Homer and the Odyssey*, 2nd edition (Oxford, 2011).

S. Schein, *Reading the Odyssey: Selected Interpretive Essays* (Princeton, 1996).

C. Segal, *Singers, Heroes and Gods in the Odyssey* (Ithaca, NY, 1994).

Chapter 1: Looking for Homer

Ancient representations of Homer

W. Burkert, 'The making of Homer in the 6th century BCE: rhapsodes versus Stesichorus', in E. Bothmer, ed., *The Amasis Painter and his World* (Malibu, CA, 1987) 43–62 (reprinted in *Kleine Schriften* I, 2001: 189–97, and in D. Cairns, ed., *Oxford Readings in Homer's Iliad*, 2001: 92–116).

B. Graziosi, *Inventing Homer: The Early Reception of Epic* (Cambridge, 2002).

W. Wallis, 'Homer: A Guide to Sculptural Types', *Living Poets* (Durham, 2015) <https://livingpoets.dur.ac.uk/w/Homer:_ A_Guide_to_Sculptural_Types>.

Ancient Homeric scholarship and the beginnings of modern Homeric scholarship

E. Dickey, *Ancient Greek Scholarship: A Guide to Finding, Reading, and Understanding Scholia, Commentaries, Lexica, and Grammatical Treatises, from their Beginnings to the Byzantine Period* (Oxford, 2007).

R. Nünlist, *The Ancient Critic at Work. Terms and Concepts of Literary Criticism in Greek Scholia* (Cambridge, 2009).

R. Pfeiffer, *History of Classical Scholarship: From the Beginnings to the End of the Hellenistic Age* (Oxford, 1968).

A. Grafton, G. W. Most, and J. E. G. Zetzel, eds, *F. A. Wolf: Prolegomena to Homer, 1795* (Princeton, 1985).

Chapter 2: Textual clues

Oral poetry

E. Bakker, *Pointing at the Past: From Formula to Performance in Homeric Poetics* (Cambridge, MA, 2005).

J. M. Bremer, I. de Jong, and J. Kalff, eds, *Homer: Beyond Oral Poetry. Recent Trends in Homeric Interpretation* (Amsterdam, 1987).

J. M. Foley, *Homer's Traditional Art* (University Park, PA, 1999).

A. Lord, *The Singer of Tales*, 2nd edition with CD-Rom, eds S. Mitchell and G. Nagy (Cambridge, MA, 2000).

G. Nagy, *Poetry as Performance: Homer and Beyond* (Cambridge, 1996).

G. Nagy, *Plato's Rhapsody and Homer's Music: The Poetics of the Panathenaic Festival in Classical Athens* (Washington, DC, 2002).

M. Parry, *The Making of Homeric Verse: The Collected Papers of Milman Parry*, ed. A. Parry (Oxford, 1971).

Homeric language and grammar

Ø. Andersen and D. T. T. Haug, eds, *Relative Chronology in Early Greek Epic Poetry* (Cambridge, 2012).

P. Chantraine, *Grammaire Homérique* (Paris, 1948–53).

R. Janko, *Homer, Hesiod and the Hymns: Diachronic Development in Epic Diction* (Cambridge, 1982).

D. B. Monro, *A Grammar of the Homeric Dialect* (Oxford, 1891; repr. Bristol, 1998).

B. Snell et al. *Lexikon des frühgriechischen Epos* (Göttingen, 1955–2010).

J. R. Tebben, *Concordantia Homerica, Pars 1: Odyssea. A Computer Concordance to the van Thiel Edition of Homer's Odyssey* (Hildesheim, 1994).

J. R. Tebben, *Concordantia Homerica, Pars 2: Ilias. A Computer Concordance to the van Thiel Edition of Homer's Iliad* (Hildesheim, 1998).

Early texts of Homer

A. C. Cassio, 'Early editions of the Greek epics and Homeric textual criticism', in F. Montanari, ed., *Omero tremila anni dopo* (Rome, 2002), 105–36.

Chapter 3: Material clues

C. Antonaccio, *An Archaeology of Ancestors: Tomb Cult and Hero Cult in Ancient Greece* (Lanham, MD, 1994).

M. Finkelberg, *Greeks and Pre-Greeks: Aegean Prehistory and Greek Heroic Tradition* (Cambridge, 2005).

I. Malkin, *The Returns of Odysseus: Colonisation and Ethnicity* (Berkeley, 1998).

I. Morris, *Archaeology as Cultural History: Words and Things in Iron Age Greece* (Malden, MA, 2000).

B. B. Powell, *Homer and the Origin of the Greek Alphabet* (Cambridge, 1991).

J. Neils, *Goddess and Polis: The Panathenaic Festival in Ancient Athens* (Princeton, 1992).

J. I. Porter, 'Making and unmaking: the Achaean Wall and the limits of fictionality in Homeric criticism', *Transactions of the American Philological Association* 141 (2011): 1–36.

C. Runnels, *The Archaeology of Heinrich Schliemann: An Annotated Bibliographic Handlist* (Boston, 2002).

Chapter 4: The poet in the poems

S. Goldhill, *The Poet's Voice: Essays on Poetics and Greek Literature* (Cambridge, 1991).

B. Graziosi, 'The poet in the *Iliad*', in A. Marmodoro and J. Hill, eds, *The Author's Voice in Classical and Late Antiquity* (Oxford, 2013) 9–38.

I. de Jong and R. Nünlist, 'From bird's eye view to close-up: the standpoint of the narrator in the Homeric epics', in A. Bierl, A. Schmitt, and A. Willi, eds, *Antike Literatur in neuer Deutung. Festschrift für Joachim Latacz anlässlich seines 70. Geburtstages* (Munich, 2004) 63–83.

E. Minchin, *Homer and the Resources of Memory: Some Applications of Cognitive Theory to the Iliad and the Odyssey* (Oxford, 2001).

A. Purves, *Space and Time in Ancient Greek Narrative* (Cambridge, 2010).

S. D. Richardson, *The Homeric Narrator* (Nashville, 1990).

R. Scodel, *Listening to Homer: Tradition, Narrative, and Audience* (Ann Arbor, 2002).

J. Strauss Clay, *Homer's Trojan Theater: Space, Vision, and Memory in the Iliad* (Cambridge, 2011).

M. M. Winkler, ed., *Troy: from Homer's Iliad to Hollywood Epic* (Oxford, 2007).

Chapter 5: The wrath of Achilles

D. Cairns, *Aidōs: The Psychology and Ethics of Honour and Shame in Ancient Greek Literature* (Oxford, 1993).

M. Clarke, *Flesh and Spirit in the Songs of Homer: A Study of Words and Myths* (Oxford, 1999).

D. Elmer, *The Poetics of Consent: Collective Decision Making in the Iliad* (Baltimore, 2012).

J. Griffin, 'Homeric words and speakers', *Journal of Hellenic Studies* 106 (1986): 36–57.

L. Muellner, *The Anger of Achilles: Mênis in Greek Epic* (Ithaca, NY, 1996).

L. Slatkin, *The Power of Thetis: Allusion and Interpretation in the Iliad* (Berkeley, 1991).

G. Zanker, *The Heart of Achilles: Characterization and Personal Ethics in the Iliad* (Ann Arbor, 1994).

Chapter 6: A poem about Troy

J. Griffin, *Homer on Life and Death* (Oxford, 1980), esp. chapter 4.

J. Haubold, *Homer's People: Epic Poetry and Social Formation* (Cambridge, 2000).

S. Scully, *Homer and the Sacred City* (Ithaca, NY, 1990).

Chapter 7: The tragedy of Hector

M. Alexiou, *The Ritual Lament in Greek Tradition*, revised edition
  D. Yatromanolakis and P. Roilos (Lanham, MD, 2002).

M. Arthur Katz, 'The divided world of *Iliad* VI', in H. Foley, ed.,
  Reflections of Women in Antiquity (New York, 1981), 19–44.

P. E. Easterling, 'The tragic Homer', *Bulletin of the Institute of
  Classical Studies* 31 (1984): 1–8.

P. E. Easterling, 'Men's κλέος and women's γόος: female voices in the
  Iliad', *Journal of Modern Greek Studies* 9 (1991): 145–51.

B. Graziosi and J. Haubold, eds, *Homer: Iliad VI* (Cambridge, 2010).

I. de Jong, ed., *Homer: Iliad XXII* (Cambridge, 2012).

C. W. MacLeod, *Homer: Iliad XXIV* (Cambridge, 1982).

J. Redfield, *Nature and Culture in the Iliad: The Tragedy of Hector*,
  2nd edition (Durham, NC, 1994).

J. Strauss Clay, 'Dying is hard to do', *Colby Quarterly* 38.1 (2002): 7–16.

Chapter 8: The man of many turns

M. Detienne and J.-P. Vernant, *Cunning Intelligence in Greek Culture
  and Society*, trans. J. Lloyd (Chicago, 1991).

G. W. Most, 'The structure and function of Odysseus' *Apologoi*',
  Transactions of the American Philological Association 199 (1989):
  15–30.

M. Nagler, 'Odysseus: the proem and the problem', *Classical Antiquity*
  9 (1990): 335–56.

J. Peradotto, *Man in the Middle Voice: Name and Narration in the
  Odyssey* (Princeton, 1990).

L. H. Pratt, *Lying and Poetry from Homer to Pindar* (Ann Arbor, 1993).

P. Pucci, 'The proem of the *Odyssey*', *Arethusa* 15 (1982): 39–62.

D. Steiner, ed., *Homer: Odyssey XVII–XVIII* (Cambridge, 2010).

Chapter 9: Women and monsters

L. G. Canevaro, *Women of Substance in Homeric Epic: Women,
  Objects, Agency* (Oxford, 2018).

B. Clayton, *A Penelopean Poetics: Reweaving the Feminine in Homer's
  Odyssey* (Lanham, MD, 2004).

N. Felson-Rubin, *Regarding Penelope: From Character to Poetics*
  (Princeton, 1994).

A. F. Garvie, *Homer: Odyssey VI–VIII* (Cambridge, 1994).

M. Katz, *Penelope's Renown: Meaning and Indeterminacy in the Odyssey* (Princeton, 1991).

J. Redfield, 'The economic man', in C. A. Rubino and C. W. Shelmerdine, eds, *Approaches to Homer* (Austin, 1983), 218–47, reprinted in L. E. Doherty, ed., *Oxford Readings in Homer's Odyssey* (Oxford, 2009): 265–87.

J. Strauss Clay, *The Wrath of Athena: Gods and Men in the Odyssey*, corrected reprint (Lanham, MD, 1997).

T. van Nortwick, 'Penelope and Nausicaa', *Transactions of the American Philological Association* 109 (1979): 269–76.

Chapter 10: An infernal journey

G. Gazis, *Homer and the Poetics of Hades* (Oxford, 2018).

B. Graziosi and E. Greenwood, *Homer in the Twentieth Century: Between World Literature and the Western Canon* (Oxford, 2007).

E. Hall, *The Return of Ulysses: A Cultural History of Homer's Odyssey* (London, 2008).

J. D. Reid, ed., *The Oxford Guide to Classical Mythology in the Arts, 1300–1990s* (Oxford, 1993).

W. B. Stanford, *The Ulysses Theme: A Study in the Adaptability of a Traditional Hero*, 2nd edition (Oxford, 1963).

Index

SOCIAL MEDIA
Very Short Introduction

Join our community

www.oup.com/vsi

- Join us online at the official Very Short Introductions **Facebook** page.
- Access the thoughts and musings of our authors with our online **blog**.
- Sign up for our monthly **e-newsletter** to receive information on all new titles publishing that month.
- Browse the full range of Very Short Introductions online.
- Read **extracts** from the Introductions for free.
- If you are a teacher or lecturer you can order inspection copies quickly and simply via our website.

CLASSICAL MYTHOLOGY
A Very Short Introduction
Helen Morales

From Zeus and Europa, to Diana, Pan, and Prometheus, the myths of ancient Greece and Rome seem to exert a timeless power over us. But what do those myths represent, and why are they so enduringly fascinating? This imaginative and stimulating *Very Short Introduction* is a wide-ranging account, examining how classical myths are used and understood in both high art and popular culture, taking the reader from the temples of Crete to skyscrapers in New York, and finding classical myths in a variety of unexpected places: from Arabic poetry and Hollywood films, to psychoanalysis, the bible, and New Age spiritualism.

www.oup.com/vsi

LATE ANTIQUITY
A Very Short Introduction
Gillian Clark

Late antiquity is the period (c.300–c.800) in which barbarian invasions ended Roman Empire in Western Europe by the fifth century and Arab invasions ended Roman rule over the eastern and southern Mediterranean coasts by the seventh century. Asking 'what, where, and when' Gillian Clark presents an introduction to the concept of late antiquity and the events of its time. Not only a period of cultural clashes, political restructurings, and geographical controversies, Clark also demonstrates the sheer richness and diversity of religious life as well as the significant changes to trade, economy, archaeology, and towns. Encapsulating significant developments through vignettes, she reflects upon the period by asking the question 'How much can we recognise in the world of late antiquity?'

www.oup.com/vsi

ISLAMIC HISTORY
A Very Short Introduction
Adam J. Silverstein

Does history matter? This book argues not that history matters, but that Islamic history does. This *Very Short Introduction* introduces the story of Islamic history; the controversies surrounding its study; and the significance that it holds - for Muslims and for non-Muslims alike. Opening with a lucid overview of the rise and spread of Islam, from the seventh to twenty first century, the book charts the evolution of what was originally a small, localised community of believers into an international religion with over a billion adherents. Chapters are also dedicated to the peoples - Arabs, Persians, and Turks - who shaped Islamic history, and to three representative institutions - the mosque, jihad, and the caliphate - that highlight Islam's diversity over time.

> 'The book is extremely lucid, readable, sensibly organised, and wears its considerable learning, as they say, 'lightly'.'
>
> BBC History Magazine